GOD AND THE ATHEIST

A lawyer assesses the evidence for the existence of God.

Paul Ferguson

Ambassador International
GREENVILLE, SOUTH CAROLINA & BELFAST, NORTHERN IRELAND

GOD AND THE ATHEIST

First Edition: June 2005
Second Edition: July 2005
Third Edition: March 2007

The publisher has acknowledged copyright holders for various quotations within this book. These quotations comply with the copyright principle of fair comment or fair usage.

All Scripture references are from the King James Version of the Bible

ISBN 978 1 932307 72 6

Cover Design & Page Layout by
David Siglin of A&E Media

Published by the Ambassador Group

Ambassador International
427 Wade Hampton Blvd.
Greenville, SC 29609, USA
www.emeraldhouse.com

Ambassador Productions Ltd.
Providence House
Ardenlee Street
Belfast
BT6 8QJ
Northern Ireland
www.ambassador_productions.com

The colophon is a trademark of Ambassador

WE TAKE THE SIDE OF SCIENCE IN SPITE OF THE PATENT ABSURDITY OF SOME OF ITS CONSTRUCTS, in spite of its failure to fulfill many of its extravagant promises of health and life, in spite of the tolerance of the scientific community for unsubstantiated just-so stories, because we have a prior commitment, a commitment to materialism.

It is not that the methods and institutions of science somehow compel us to accept a material explanation of the phenomenal world, but, on the contrary, that we are forced by our a priori adherence to material causes to create an apparatus of investigation and a set of concepts that produce material explanations, no matter how counter-intuitive, no matter how mystifying to the uninitiated. Moreover, that materialism is an absolute, for we cannot allow a Divine Foot in the door.

Richard Lewontin, a physicist, writing in the New York Times Book Review ("Billions and Billions of Demons")

MAN CAN CERTAINLY FLEE FROM GOD...BUT HE CANNOT ESCAPE HIM. He can certainly hate God and be hateful to God, but he cannot change into its opposite the eternal love of God which triumphs even in his hate.

Karl Barth, Christian Theologian

DEDICATION

To Rev. Dr. Peter Ng, Singapore and Dr. Napier Malcolm, Bristol who by their selfless humility and love for the Saviour daily inspires me.

To Dr. H.T. Spence who has taught me to love and respect the Bible as the greatest book in the world.

To the Henderson Family in Liverpool: true friends indeed.

To our little Mei En: the beautiful gift God has given us

8

 ACKNOWLEDGEMENTS

With the supportive help of many, the third edition of this book has been published. My grateful thanks to them all.

I owe a huge debt of gratitude to those who read and checked the logic, theology and scientific accuracy of this book. My grateful thanks to the publisher: Dr. Sam Lowry and his colleagues at Ambassador Press Intl for making this edition possible.

My grateful thanks to my esteemed teacher, Dr. H.T. Spence, a true Biblical Scholar, and friend for writing the foreword.

In addition, my grateful thanks to my beloved Pastor, Rev. Dr. Peter Ng of Jesus Saves Mission in Singapore, Zion Tabernacle in Chester, and Magherafelt Free Presbyterian Church in N.Ireland for their support. Through their generosity, thousands of copies of this book have gone freely into Communist countries.

Finally, I offer this book as a heartfelt offer of praise and worship to the God who created, loved and saved me. For, this God who made this whole world of trillions of planets in six days simply by the word of His power daily fills me with awe and wonder.

To Him and His Son we join the celestial chorus and cry:

> Salvation to our God which sitteth upon the throne, and unto the Lamb.... Blessing, and glory, and wisdom, and thanksgiving, and honour, and power, and might, be unto our God for ever and ever. Amen.
> Revelation 7:10;12

Paul Ferguson
Foundations Bible College & Theological Seminary
January 2007

TABLE OF CONTENTS

Foreword by Dr. H.T. Spence 10

Introduction 11

Part 1: HOW DO WE KNOW THERE IS A GOD?

A Question of Evidence 14

Cosmological Argument: Discovering old relatives 16

Divine Design Argument: Outbreak of the Flew 22

Morality Argument: What exactly is your question? 34

Consciousness Argument: To be or not to be? 42

Meaning of Life Argument: A hero or a fool? 47

The Verdict 52

Part 2: HOW DO WE KNOW THERE IS ONLY ONE GOD?

What kind of God do we worship? 60

Part 3: HOW DO WE KNOW THE BIBLE IS THE WORD OF GOD?

Let the Bible Speak 66

Bible & Science 69

The Bible, Prophecy & History 75

The Phenomenon of Jesus Christ 79

Part 4: WHAT DOES GOD SAY ABOUT YOU?

The Six Facts of Life 86

Part 5: APPENDICES

Testimonies of Faith 92

The Professor and the Christian 93

The Preacher and the Atheist 98

Recommended Further Reading List 100

Numerical References 101

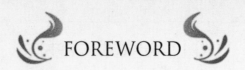 FOREWORD

The powers of secular humanism, the side effects of radical theology (theothanatology), and the ever-increasing belief of a closed-world system have brought bolder attacks against belief in the existence of God in our generation. This contemporary materialistic age has philosophically popularized the identification of being an agnostic or an atheist. It has become "academic" to denounce the existence of God and to be an evolutionist in all the social sciences of epistemology. Consequently, secular Western Civilization has become atheistic in belief and life.

In God and the Atheist, Paul Ferguson has aptly and soundly offered an honorable, apologetic defense concerning the existence of God. When verbosity often overwhelms a literary defense obscuring the potent truth of the matter, his book concisely and cogently strikes at the heart of this crucial a priori truth. Even to contemplate the Christian Faith, the individual must first believe that "he [God] is" (Hebrews 11:6a) and "he is a rewarder of them that diligently seek him" (Hebrews 11:6b).

May this book prove to be not only a conscience-probing defense to anyone who identifies himself as an agnostic or an atheist, but also a strengthening of heart and mind to the believer concerning the God of Scripture.

Dr. H. T. Spence
President, Foundations Bible College & Theological Seminary
Dunn, North Carolina

 INTRODUCTION

"Christianity is only for old people and those with a poor education," declared confidently a young Chinese student in my classroom in February 2005.

"Governments use Christianity to control their people and it hinders scientific and economic advancement," she continued. The two Vietnamese students seated beside her nodded confidently in agreement.

"How do you explain then the fact that the USA is the most scientifically and economically advanced nation on earth, yet 95% of Americans believe in God?"[1] I replied.

"If there is a God, then prove He exists," they challenged ignoring my question.

"If I could prove the evidence for God's existence is factually and logically overwhelming, would you be prepared to acknowledge Him?" I replied.

Three months later, the same three students sat around the communion table of my church in Singapore with my wife and I, having received the free gift of eternal life through Jesus Christ alone and having acknowledged the One True God as their Creator. This work is really a by-product of their testimonies[2] and of many other students who have been taught uncritically that atheism is a fact – only to have their pre-suppositions "shot down in flames" when tested by the laws of logic and evidence.

The evidence set out in summary form below may evidentially satisfy the proposition that God exists but the wonderful thing about Christianity is that I cannot make you accept it. The evidence can satisfy your intellect but only you can exercise your will to accept Jesus Christ as your personal Saviour.

If you don't like the exclusive claims of Christianity that there is only one God and that Jesus is the only way to heaven, remember I did not write them – God did.[3] All I am doing is simply presenting them.

As you read this book remember as every second passes on average two people will have just died and during today some 150,000 people will have died around the world! Tomorrow you could be one of them. If you are an atheist, you will have the most important decision of your life to make when you come to the end of this book. So, if you have your brain switched on and want to hear the case for the evidence for God's existence, read on!

In this study we will seek to answer three common questions posed by atheists in challenging Christianity:

1. How do we know that there is a God?
2. How do we know that there is only one God?
3. How do we know the Bible is the Word of God?

I hope and pray that this message will reach many more lives so that they may see that the religion of the Church of Atheism is truly a "non-prophet organization." As in all good apologetics, we will simply use the critical thinking skills we were born with and let the "world's most indestructible best-seller"[4] speak - the Bible.

Part 1

HOW DO WE KNOW THERE IS A GOD?

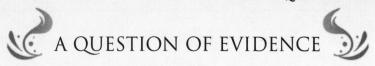

A QUESTION OF EVIDENCE

THE MORE I STUDY SCIENCE, THE MORE I BELIEVE IN GOD.
Albert Einstein

Atheism is defined as the "disbelief in the existence of God or gods."[5]
Theism, by contrast, is the "belief in the existence of God or gods."[6]

This certitude of atheistic belief is incredible when you consider
that even prominent atheists like Thomas Edison admit: "We don't
know a millionth of one percent about anything." Indeed, we still don't
know what 90% of the universe is made of. What is gravity? What are
the fundamental particles of matter such as electrons, quarks, protons
composed of? What is energy? Why is it a gram of rose petals contains
an identical amount[7] of energy as a gram of uranium? We don't even
know how these things work let alone why. It certainly therefore takes
faith to be an atheist.

"But you cannot see God," a student complained to me. "True,"
I replied, "but you cannot see electrons, music, magnetic fields, your
mind or the wind, yet you do not doubt their existence." The Russian
astronaut, Major Gherman Titov, who on August 7, 1961 became the
second man to orbit the earth, boasted when attending the World's Fair
that he had looked around space "very attentively" but had not seen
God or any angels. His comments led someone to wittily reply: "Had he
stepped out of his space-suit he would have!"

Another common complaint is that there is not enough evidence
for the existence of God. The famous atheistic philosopher Bertrand
Russell was once asked, "If you meet God after you die, what will you
say to Him to justify your unbelief?"

"I will tell Him that He did not give me enough evidence," Russell
proudly replied. The Bible tells us unequivocally that there is more than
enough evidence to show God exists.

For the invisible things of him from the creation of the world are
clearly seen, being understood by the things that are made, even his
eternal power and Godhead; so that they are without excuse:
Romans 1:20

The problem isn't about lack of evidence but simply a suppression
or willful neglect of the evidence. As Abraham Lincoln said:

I can see how it might be possible for a man to look down upon the earth and be an atheist, but I cannot conceive how he could look up into the heavens and say there is no God

In this book we will evaluate some of this evidence but we cannot do anything about the stubborn pride of a man like Prof. Thomas Nagel of New York University who said:

I want atheism to be true and am made uneasy by the fact that some of the most intelligent and well-informed people I know are religious believers. It isn't just that I don't believe in God and, naturally, hope that I'm right in my belief. It's that I hope there is no God! I don't want there to be a God; I don't want the universe to be like that.[8]

Often the charge that is leveled against Christians is that they blindly believe in faith. This claim pre-supposes that atheists alone are the guardians of reason in contrast to those "irrational religionists." The truth is that our whole lives are based on faith. We have faith that our dentist and doctor are qualified to treat us, we have faith that the brakes in our car will work when we apply them, we have faith that our milk and sugar in our cornflakes have been produced to the standards claimed by the manufacturers. You cannot live life without faith.

David Hume, the eighteenth century philosopher, railed against theism boasting that the test for anything meaningful was:

Does it contain any abstract reasoning concerning quantity or number? No. Does it contain any experimental reasoning concerning matter of fact and existence? No. Commit it to the flames; for it can contain nothing but sophistry and illusion.[9]

The irony here for Hume is that his own test does not pass the test! If to be meaningful a belief has to be numerically or scientifically verified, then Hume's test is meaningless as it cannot be verified in this way. So, before committing the Bible to the flames, perhaps Hume should light it with his own books! It takes just as much faith to be an atheist (indeed, more as we will show in this book) than to believe in God. For to be atheistic concerning religious beliefs requires the atheist being a believer in a completely different series of beliefs!

In English Criminal law a defendant cannot be convicted for a crime unless the burden of proof against them is "beyond reasonable doubt." This is a high standard of proof but I am confident the overwhelming evidence for the existence of God satisfies this test. If we cannot see

God, then we should evaluate the evidence for His existence using the same method we use to discover those things that we cannot see, namely their effects.

There are diverse and complicated arguments to evidence the proposition that God exists. In this book, however, we will only look at a summary of five of the simpler to understand of these. For those interested in a more substantive study of these arguments a list of recommended books for further study is set out in Appendix 4.

COSMOLOGICAL ARGUMENT: DISCOVERING OLD RELATIVES

THE USUAL APPROACH OF SCIENCE of constructing a mathematical model cannot answer the questions of why there should be a universe for the model to describe. Why does the universe go to all the bother of existing?
Stephen Hawking

In 1916 a young German born scientist of Jewish extraction called Albert Einstein published a paper detailing a new theory of the origin of the universe. Einstein, who had mixed educational success growing up (having once failed an exam to qualify as a teacher), held a research position in the Prussian Academy of Sciences together with a non-teaching chair at the University of Berlin. His paper was to have monumental historical significance and would make Einstein world famous.

Einstein's mathematical theorem of General Relativity suggested that the known universe is expanding and had a definite beginning to all time, all space and all matter. Before that, nothing existed and the laws of physics break down. Up to this time, atheists had clung to the idea that the universe was eternal. Einstein's theorem was to have devastating implications for this much cherished belief. After Einstein published his Theory of General Relativity (TGR) many scientists, including Einstein (who called it "irritating"), were unhappy with the implications of his discovery, as they wanted to believe the Universe never had a beginning. When British eclipse expeditions in 1919 appeared to confirm his predictions, Einstein was hailed as a genius by the popular press.

In 1927 Einstein's theory achieved international scientific recognition when astronomer Edwin Hubble was the first to actually observe the expansion of the universe through his 100-inch telescope at Mount Wilson Astronomy in California. Hubble recorded observing a discernable difference in the colour of light from different galaxies within 6x1O17 miles of the Earth was receding over time. This was substantive evidence that the galaxies were moving apart and the universe was expanding. Even Einstein was forced to admit, albeit reluctantly: "New observations by Hubble . . . make it appear likely that the general structure of the universe is not static."

Today most scientists now accept that the vast bulk of observational scientific evidence supports TGR, which implies the universe had a beginning and is expanding! Leading atheist, Anthony Flew in a debate in 1998 speaking about TGR admits this and states:

If it was a matter of my preference, I would certainly prefer a cyclical universe exploding and contracting, and so on. This idea has apparently been empirically ruled out…it is certainly the dominant theory today and the one, therefore, we have to work with.[10]

TGR is one of the strongest pieces of evidence for what is referred to traditionally by philosophers as the Cosmological Argument.

The Cosmological Argument is simply the argument from the beginning of the world. The form of this argument is relatively straightforward.

1. Whatever begins to exist has a cause for its coming into being.
2. The universe had a beginning.
3. Therefore, the universe has a cause for its coming into being.

The fundamental basis for modern science is the Law of Causality, which simply expresses that everything that had a beginning had a cause. It is conceptually similar to the statement that whatever has an effect has a cause. If we didn't have this law, then all science would be meaningless for science is fundamentally a search for causes. If someone tells you they don't believe in this law, simply ask them "What caused you to come to that conclusion?"

Some sceptics claim that Premise 1 is wrong and maybe something comes from nothing! Imagine if Christians taught such absurd theology.

We would be mocked in every newspaper and science journal with "join the church that believes trillions of stars came from nothing by nothing!" or referred derisively as the church with a holy book that says: "in the beginning nothing created something."

Atheist philosopher, Prof. Kai Nielsen sums it up rather well when he illustrates:

> Suppose you suddenly hear a loud bang…and you ask me, "What caused that bang?" And I reply, "Nothing, it just happened." You would not accept that. In fact, you would find my reply quite unintelligible.[11]

So, if Premise 1 is incontrovertibly true can we show that Premise 2 is also and the universe had a beginning?

Second Law of Thermodynamics

"I just don't believe I can beat Father Time," declared the 38 year old former boxing heavyweight champion of the world "Iron" Mike Tyson as he announced his retirement on June 2005.[12] Tyson illustrated well by his comments the effects of the Second Law of Thermodynamics on a human. This law states in simple terms that the universe is running out of useable energy and all things are growing older, wearing out, becoming more disordered and decaying. We all know, for instance, that heat spontaneously flows from a hot body to a cold one (never the reverse), flowers wither, iron rusts, colours fade, men die, everything will eventually degenerate. There is no known exception to this law. Dr. Norman Geisler explains the significance of this law to theistic belief:

> The First Law of Thermodynamics states that the total amount of energy in the universe is constant. In other words, the universe has only a finite amount or energy (much as your car has only a finite amount of gas). Now, if your car has only a finite amount of gas (the First Law), and whenever it's running it continually consumes gas (the Second Law), would your car be running right now if you had started it up an infinitely long time ago? No, of course not. It would have run out of gas. In the same way, the universe would be running out of energy by now if it had been running from all eternity. But here we are – the lights are still on, so the universe must have begun in the finite past. That is, the universe is not eternal – it must have had a beginning.[13]

Also, if our universe is becoming less ordered – then where did the original order come from? For, if the naturalistic blind process of chance universally results in progressive disorder, how could this same process logically account for the universe's original state of optimal order?

Indeed, why are there orderly laws? Why not chaos? For if atheists struggle to explain how nothing produces something, then they will have even greater difficulty explaining how natural laws could come from nothing that give rise to purposeful and highly specific achievements.

Radioactivity

Chemistry has shown that radioactive elements decay over time until in the end they become a different element. We know, for example, that radioactive uranium eventually ionizes into lead. However, if all the uranium atoms were infinitely old, surely they would all have been converted into lead? As this has clearly not happened, we can conclude the universe is not infinitely old.

Conclusion

Founder of NASA's Goddard Institute of Space Studies and arguably the greatest astrophysicist of his time Robert Jastrow, a self-proclaimed agnostic, appropriately described what has happened to his sceptical colleagues as they have measured the cosmos:

> Now we see how the astronomical evidence leads to a biblical view of the origin of the world....for the scientist who has lived by his faith in the power of reason, the story ends like a bad dream. He has scaled the mountains of ignorance; he is about to conquer the highest peak; as he pulls himself over the final rock, he is greeted by a band of theologians who have been sitting there for centuries.[14]

The evidence that the world had a beginning is now so overwhelming that even the strongest atheists have accepted it, albeit with bad grace. Einstein's contemporary and British cosmologist, Arthur Eddington wrote of it:

> Philosophically, the notion of a beginning of the present order of nature is repugnant to me...I should like to find a genuine loophole....it leaves me cold.[15]

Unfortunately for atheists, there is no loophole as Eddington was forced to admit: "The beginning seems to present insuperable difficulties unless we agree to look on it as frankly supernatural."[16]

Jastrow also commented on the Bible and the scientific evidence:

> The astronomical evidence leads to a biblical view of the origin of the world. The details differ, but the essential elements in the astronomical and the biblical accounts of Genesis are the same. The chain of events leading to man commenced suddenly and sharply at a definite moment in time, in a flash of light and energy.

So overwhelming is the cosmological argument for the existence of God that it has been reported that many scientists have renounced atheism. Newsweek reported a sharp increase of belief in theism by scientists in a 1998 edition: "Forty percent of American scientists now believe in a personal God - not merely an ineffable power and presence in the world, but a deity to whom they can pray."[17]

Indeed, Newsweek columnist, George Will began his November 9, 1998 column by joking:

> Soon the American Civil Liberties Union, or People for the American Way, or some similar faction of litigious secularism will file suit against NASA, charging that the Hubble Space Telescope unconstitutionally gives comfort to the religiously inclined.

Cosmological science has now provided abundant evidence that our universe had a beginning. This beginning now requires an explanation. We can conclude from the cosmological evidence that the First Cause of the universe must be self-existent, immaterial, timeless or eternal and nonspatial – since the First Cause created all of these.

Some sceptics ask: "Then, who made God?"

Remember, the Law of Causality states that everything that has a beginning has a cause. God is outside space, time, and matter as He did not have a beginning, so He therefore does not need a cause!

We cannot fully comprehend a person like God who is outside all time, all space and all matter (it hurts our head to try). How can we the finite mind comprehend the infinite? For instance, we may think we can conceptualise the end of all space in the universe, as set out in the TGR, but if we were to travel there – what would be behind it?

Robert Jastrow explained why so many atheistic scientists refuse to bow to the inevitable:

Scientists cannot bear the thought of a natural phenomenon which cannot be explained, even with unlimited time and money. There is a kind of religion in science; every event can be explained in a rational way as the product of some previous event; every effect must have its cause. Now science ....asks, "What cause produced this effect? Who or what put the matter into the universe? And science cannot answer these questions."

A good example of this refusal to accept the obvious was John Echols, a Nobel laureate in neurophysiology, who said in 1968:

The odds are against the right combinations of circumstances occurring to evolve intelligent life on earth. The odds are about 400,000 trillion trillion trillion trillion to one. Evolution is fantastically improbable. I believe that it did occur, but that it could never occur again on any planet or any other solar system. Now, that is Faith!

Who hath measured the waters in the hollow of his hand, and meted out heaven with the span, and comprehended the dust of the earth in a measure, and weighed the mountains in scales, and the hills in a balance?

Who hath directed the Spirit of the LORD, or being his counsellor hath taught him?

With whom took he counsel, and who instructed him, and taught him in the path of judgment, and taught him knowledge, and shewed to him the way of understanding?

Behold, the nations are as a drop of a bucket, and are counted as the small dust of the balance: behold, he taketh up the isles as a very little thing.

All nations before him are as nothing; and they are counted to him less than nothing, and vanity.

To whom then will ye liken God? or what likeness will ye compare unto him?

Isaiah 40:12-18

DIVINE DESIGN ARGUMENT: OUTBREAK OF THE FLEW

THE GOD OF THE BIBLE IS ALSO THE GOD OF THE GENOME . . . . He can be
worshiped in the cathedral or in the laboratory.
-Dr. Francis Collins

Late in 2004, shock waves resounded through the world of atheism as a leading atheistic philosopher, Anthony Flew indicated a change of mind about theism. One of the newspapers covering the story, The Times of London referred to Flew as "one of the most renowned atheists of the past half-century, whose papers and lectures have formed the bedrock of unbelief for many adherents."

Flew, although born the son of a Christian clergyman, was a champion of atheism in debates and books for most of his 81 years. He acknowledged the persuasive nature of intelligent design as compelling evidence for the existence of a Creator God. In an interview with Christianity Today,[18] Flew stated his acceptance of an intelligent designer of the universe and cited his affinity with Einstein who believed in "an Intelligence that produced the integrative complexity of creation." Einstein openly affirmed his belief in an intelligent designer:

> We are in the position of a little child entering a huge library filled with books in many different languages. The child knows someone must have written those books. It does not know how. It does not understand the languages in which they are written. The child dimly suspects a mysterious order in the arrangement of the books but doesn't know what it is. That seems to me, is the attitude of even the most intelligent being toward God. We see a universe marvellously arranged and obeying certain laws, but only dimly understand those laws. Our limited minds cannot grasp the mysterious force that moves the constellations.[19]

The form of this argument is also simple and straightforward.

1. All designs have a designer.
2. The universe has highly complex design.
3. Therefore, the universe has a designer.

The most famous advocate of the design argument was William Paley who, writing in the eighteenth century, illustrated this with the example of someone finding a watch while walking in the countryside. Paley argued that because the watch had designed features such as spring, gearwheels, pointer, it was only logical to conclude that it had a maker who "comprehended its construction and designed its use." Paley applied this analogy to the evidence of design in the eye and other organs of the body to imply an intelligent Creator.

As science has discovered more about the universe we are beginning to understand just how incredibly complex the design of this universe is. Overall, the universe seems perfectly ordered to facilitate life, personality, critical thinking and reasoning. Even to the casual observer, the order and beauty of nature touches something deep within us and fills us with awe.

It is important to note when we refer to "intelligent design" through-out this study, we are not speaking necessarily of optimality or perfection of design but simply referring to "intelligent" agency (irrespective of the skill of the designer). Theology has provided the answer why some things in the universe may have increasingly sub-optimal or less than perfect designs.[20] Ironically, those atheists who point to sub-optimal designs in the universe imply that they know what optimal design is and therefore intelligent design is observable and testable.

In all other fields of human experience we find that design necessitates a designer. It is also important to note at this point that making design inferences is an established and a fundamental part of modern science. We see this in many disciplines, including archaeology, anthropology, forensics, criminal jurisprudence, copyright law, patent law, reverse engineering, crypto-analysis, random number generation, and even to the search for extraterrestrial intelligence (SETI). Indeed, the logic of the latter search led Dr. Charles B. Thaxton, a Postdoctoral Fellow in Chemistry at Harvard University to comment:

An intelligible communication via radio signal from some distant galaxy would be widely hailed as evidence of an intelligent source. Why then doesn't the message sequence on the DNA molecule also constitute prima facie evidence for an intelligent source? After all, DNA information is not just analogous to a message sequence such as Morse code, it is such a message sequence.[21]

We can infer intelligent design because it leaves distinctive hallmarks that in the complete realm of human experience point to an intelligent cause. Therefore, we can infer design in the examples below based on what we know of the distinctive signature of intelligent agents. Put simply, it is the only credible show in town that adequately explains how we have designs and complexities in our universe that exceed enormously those we know are produced by agents of intelligent design. Chance can explain complexity, but not specification.

If we have a logical and credible explanation, why should we search for some "magical" natural selection process to try to explain this design complexity? As Geisler explains:

The central principle in forensic science is the Principle of Uniformity, which holds that causes in the past were like the causes we observe today. In other words, by the Principle of Uniformity, we assume that the world worked in the past just like it works today, especially when it comes to causes. If a coded message requires an intelligent cause today, then any similar message from the past must also require an intelligent cause. Conversely, if natural laws can do the job today, then the Principle of Uniformity would lead us to conclude natural laws could do the job in the past.[22]

The Bible says in Proverbs 3:19—"The LORD by wisdom hath founded the earth; by understanding hath he established the heavens."

Let us now look at see if the complexity and specification of design in nature matches up to this claim.

Cell

Cells are the fundamental building block of life. We have approximately 100 trillion of them. Until the advent of molecular biology, many scientists thought the cell would be a simplistic structure. Instead, we find the complete opposite! Apart from the brain, the cell is the most complex structure in the universe. For instance, a British team discovered a cellular F1F0-ATPase enzyme with an in-built rotary engine no bigger than ten billionths by ten billionths of a metre.[23] One scientist recently described a single cell organism as a high-tech factory made up of 10 million atoms and complete with: artificial languages and their decoding systems, memory banks for information storage and retrieval, elegant control systems regulating the automated assembly of parts and components, error fail-safe and proof-reading devices utilized for quality control, assembly processes involving the principles of prefabrication and modular construction... and a capacity not equaled in any of our own most advanced machines, for it would be capable of replicating its entire structure within a matter of hours.[24]

Remember, all of us reading this started out as a single cell nine months before we were born. Nine months later this single cell had incredibly divided into trillions of cells that had differentiated into two hundred different varieties (each with differing functions such as kidney cells, brain cells, and liver cells, everything that will make us a complete functioning human). M.I.T. researcher, Dr. Gerald Schroeder illustrates:

> Each cell in your body, is selecting right now approximately five hundred thousand amino acids, consisting of some ten million atoms, organizing them into preselected strings, joining them together, checking to be certain each string is folded into specific shapes, and then shipping each protein off to a site, some inside the cell, some outside, sites that somehow have signaled a need for these specific proteins. Every second. Every cell. Your body is a living wonder.[25]

When in the history of science or engineering did such an advanced machine as the cell arise simply by "chance?" Agnostic biologist, Dr. Michael Denton agrees:

> The complexity of the simplest known type of cell is so great that it is impossible to accept that such an object could have been thrown together suddenly by some kind of freakish, vastly improbable, event. Such an occurrence would be indistinguishable from a miracle.[26]

DNA

Inside each of our 100 trillion cells there is coiled 2 metres of DNA[27] which weighs about 6 trillionths of a gram. Each cell has 30,000 genes in 23 pairs of chromosomes, which can yield as many as 20-25,000 different kinds of proteins. DNA contains vast stores of information that the cell uses to make the proteins for living. Bill Gates stated that: "DNA is like a software program, only much more complex than anything we've devised" – which raises the suggestive question why would chance create informative DNA when it cannot create any of Microsoft's programs? I don't imagine Mr. Gates has contracted "Employee No 9999 Mr. Chance" for the development of Microsoft's Next Generation Windows package even if he agrees to work for the next billion years!

Speaking of the complexity of DNA and RNA, agnostic biologist Dr. Michael Denton comments:

> It is astonishing to think that this remarkable piece of machinery, which possesses the ultimate capacity to construct every living thing that ever existed on Earth, from the giant redwood to the human brain, can construct all its own components in a matter of minutes and weigh less than 10-16grams. It is of the order of several thousand million million times smaller than the smallest piece of functional machinery ever constructed by man.[28]

The information content in DNA of one cell of the three billion codes of the human genome is equivalent to more than 75,000 copies of the New York Times newspaper. Could this information have arisen by chance through physical laws like snowflakes or crystals? Berkeley Law Professor, Philip Johnson explains:

> Information is an entirely different kind of stuff from the physical medium in which it may be temporarily recorded. It would be absurd to try to explain the literary quality or meaning of a book as an emergent property of the physical qualities of its ink and paper. The message comes from an author; ink and paper are merely the media. Similarly, the information written in DNA is not the product of DNA. Where did all the information come from? Who or what is the author?
>
> Physical laws cannot be the answer. These laws do produce some fairly complex structures, such as snowflakes and crystal. In such cases the laws produce the same structure over and over again, with chance variations. Repetitive order has a very low information content.[29]

So, if physical laws cannot produce this information because of its highly specified nature, who exactly is the author? As former atheist Prof. Anthony Flew confessed:

"I think the argument to Intelligent Design is enormously
stronger than it was when I first met it ….It now seems to me
that the findings of more than fifty years of DNA research
have provided materials for a new and enormously powerful
argument to design."[30]

It should be noted, we are talking here about evidence that life forms are
designed. We are not talking about what you know only by faith. What
convinced Flew was evidence, not faith!

Eye

The eye is one four-thousandth of an adult's weight and has 120
million photosensitive cells in the retina that translate light into nerve
impulses that reaches the brain through the optic nerve. There are
around 40,000,000 nerve endings that make up the optic nerve. In fact,
we will all blink our eyes around 400 million times during our lifetime
(try getting your windscreen wipers to do that without replacement).
If you lose your eye, the best eye surgeons in the world can only offer
you a coloured glass "marble" to cover the hole. Why? The design and
creation of an eye is beyond replication by "intelligent" scientists
today. Yet, we are supposed to believe it evolved by chance! Even Charles
Darwin admitted the difficulty of this for atheists: "To suppose that the
eye could have been formed by natural selection, seems I freely confess,
absurd in the highest degree."[31]

Brain

In 2005 IBM announced in a blaze of publicity the launching of
the world's most powerful supercomputer IBM's Blue Gene/L.[32] This
computer we are told has the equivalent processing power of the human
brain.[33]

The tough part, Dave Turek, IBM's vice president of deep com-
puting said, is interconnecting the processors "so they act like a single
human brain, rather than a collection of cells."

But human brains are still superior to supercomputers in many
respects.

Blue Gene/L has around 16 terabytes (trillion bytes) of memory; it is
estimated a brain has a 100-terabyte capacity. Brains are portable; Blue

Gene/L is the size of 64 refrigerator-size boxes covering 1,400 square feet (about the size of a tennis court). The average brain is 56 cubic inches and weighs 3.3 pounds.

The brain is a 3 pound piece of matter that has 10 billion neurons (nerve cells) with a trillion connections and can do the work of super-computers. Atheist, Isaac Asimov described it as "the most complex and orderly arrangement of matter in the universe"[34] and fellow atheist, Carl Sagan conservatively estimated:

> The equivalent of twenty million books is in the head of every one of us….The neurochemistry of the brain is astonishingly busy. The circuitry of a machine more wonderful than any devised by humans.[35]

Michael Denton explains its complexity:

> The human brain consists of about ten thousand million nerve cells. Each nerve cell puts out somewhere in the region of between ten thousand and one hundred thousand connecting fibres by which it makes contact with other nerve cells in the brain. Altogether the total number of connections in the human brain approaches 1×10^{15} or a thousand million million. ... a much greater number of specific connections than in the entire communications network on Earth.[36]

If a computer simply takes in information, processes it, stores it and gives it out (and no sane person would deny that it is the product of design and creation), then why would anyone think the infinitely more efficient and impressive brain "supercomputer" was designed and created by chance? If the building of the IBM's Blue Gene/L (which incidentally took the best minds in the world 3 years to construct) is described as "a real tour de force in engineering," [37] then why does any rational person think the brain is not also? It does not take a major extrapolation of logic to see the inductive parallel here.

As one IBM researcher ironically observed in designing the Blue Gene/L, "It's absolutely amazing, the complexity of the problem and the simplicity with which the body does it every day."

Laws of Nature

There are many laws in nature that govern the existence and main-tenance of this universe such as the Laws of Thermodynamics, Gravity and so on. This begs the obvious question: Who was the Law Giver that gave us these laws? Who maintains them? For instance every cell in our body needs to make two thousand proteins every second.

The balance of these laws and their precision we are now learning is incredible. Indeed, we read regularly in our newspapers of potential catastrophe if the earth's temperature rises by one or two degrees in temperature. For instance, if the gravitational force was altered by 0.00000000000000000000000000000000001%, our sun would not exist and neither would we![38] The most famous contemporary physicist, Prof. Stephen Hawking stated:

> The laws of science, as we know them at present, contain many fundamental numbers, like the size of the electric charge of the electron and the ratio of the masses of the proton and the electron....The remarkable fact is that the values of these numbers seem to have been very finely adjusted to make possible the development of life.[39]

Astrophysicist, Hugh Ross calculated the probability that the 122 constants of the laws of nature such as speed of light, electromagnetic force etc the earth requires to exist could exist for any planet (including earth) by chance in the universe as: one chance in 10^{138}! There are only 10^{70} atoms in the whole of the known universe![40] It should be noted that all these constants have to be present not just in the initial conditions of the universe's beginning but also throughout its existence. They do not evolve!

Does the fine-tuning of the universe imply intelligent purposeful design? British astrophysicist Sir Fred Hoyle admitted:

> A common sense interpretation of the facts suggests that a super-intellect has monkeyed with physics, as well as with chemistry and biology, and that there are no blind forces worth speaking about in nature. The numbers one calculates from the facts seem to me so overwhelming as to put this conclusion almost beyond question.[41]

As so many constants and parameters must be fine-tuned to such unimaginably precise degree, no other conclusion seems possible. Just to illustrate some of these odds. A stack of 500 sheets of paper is around two to three inches high. A stack 1×10^{24} would reach from the earth to the sun more than a million times. Astrophysicist, Michael Turner of the University of Chicago and Fermilab, describes the fine-tuning of the universe with a simile: "The precision is as if one could throw a dart across the entire universe and hit a bull's eye one millimeter in diameter on the other side." As one mathematician quipped, "Give chance a chance? No chance!"

Irreducible complexity

In 1996, a Roman Catholic Biochemist, Prof. Michael Behe struck a devastating blow to Atheistic Darwinism in the publication of his book Darwin's Black Box. The book became a best seller and the main thrust of the book was to set out the failure of Darwinism to account for the irreducible complexity found in cellular structures.

Behe illustrated this concept with the common mousetrap. A simple mousetrap has a wooden base, metal hammer, spring and metal bar to hold the hammer back when the trap is set. If any of the components are missing, then the trap fails to function and the mouse "can dance all night" on the base.

Behe demonstrated that there are numerous examples of parts of the body that cannot function without most or all its component parts being present at the same time and that each cellular structure only functions in coordination with others. For instance, DNA is mutually dependent on proteins or enzymes and the heart cannot function without the liver, lungs, brain or kidneys. Other examples include the intricate interdependent more than 20-step process of blood clotting. Prof. Behe (who is no creationist) explains the insurmountable impossibility of explaining how these all arose simultaneously:

> as biochemists have begun to examine apparently simple structures like cilia and flagella, they have discovered stagger-ing complexity, with dozens or even hundreds of precisely tai-lored parts. It is very likely that many of the parts we have not considered here are required for any cilium to function in a cell. As the number of required parts increases, the difficulty of gradually putting the system together skyrockets, and the likelihood of indirect scenarios plummets. Darwin looks more and more forlorn. ....Darwinian theory has given no explana-tion for the cilium or flagellum. The overwhelming complex-ity of these systems pushes us to think it may never give an explanation.[42]

Despite high level attempts by atheistic Darwinists to debunk Behe's thesis[43] it remains robust and so far unassailable. If Behe's hypothesis is correct it certainly would be the death knell for Charles Darwin theory of evolution as Darwin admitted that:

If it could be demonstrated that any complex organ existed which could not possibly have been formed by numerous, successive, slight modifications, my theory would absolutely break down.[44]

Sorry Mr. Darwin, it looks like you are out of business. You have failed your own test!

Conclusion

Atheistic scientists Francis Crick, Carl Sagan and L.M. Murkhin have estimated that the probability of a human evolving by chance processes alone is one chance in $10^{2,000,000,000}$. Mathematicians generally assume that anything more than one chance in 10^{50} to be outside the realms of possibility![45] Recipient of two Nobel Prizes in chemistry Ilya Prigogine summed up the scientific evidence for a Creator:

> The statistical probability that organic structures and the most precisely harmonized reactions that typify living organisms would be generated by accident, is zero.[46]

Why should we accept that unguided processes can achieve what highly educated scientists cannot manage collectively or cumulatively? Even if one scientist did manage to create an eye or a cell in a laboratory it would be self-defeating as they would have used "intelligent design" to initiate and guide the process. Einstein was so moved by the obvious design of the universe that he stated:

I want to know how God created this world. I am not interested in this or that phenomenon, in the spectrum of this or that element. I want to know His thoughts; the rest are details.

When you consider these staggering odds for chance, many people are confused why atheistic scientists blindly insist that the ordered complexity as described above does not need an intelligent designer. Is it because they can't see the evidence for design? A quick glance at their writings shows that this is not in the least true:

Richard Dawkins in trying to build a case for chance to make organs like the eye called one of his books "Climbing Mount Improbable"- he should have been honest and called it "Climbing Mount Impossible!" In another book he admitted: "Biology is the study of complicated things that gives the appearance of having been designed for a purpose."[47]

Francis Crick was so worried in case any scientist would spot the obvious that he warned: "Biologists must constantly keep in mind that what they see was not designed, but rather evolved."[48]

Roger Lewin marvelled with more than a hint of irony:

> Like Darwin, we stand in awe at the wonderful creativity of nature, with an understanding of its laws enhancing its beauty for us, not diminishing it.[49]

Harvard atheist and geneticist, Richard Lewontin openly admits atheistic science's pre-suppositional bias against intelligent design:

> We take the side of science in spite of the patent absurdity of some of its constructs, in spite of its failure to fulfill many of its extravagant promises of health and life....because we have a prior commitment, a commitment to materialism. It is not that the methods and institutions of science somehow compel us to accept a material explanation of the phenomenal world, but, on the contrary, that we are forced by our a priori adherence to material causes to create an apparatus of investigation and a set of concepts that produce material explanations, no matter how counterintuitive, no matter how mystifying to the uninitiated. Moreover that materialism is absolute for we cannot allow a Divine foot in the door[50] (emphasis added).

What Dr. Lewontin is simply saying is that no matter what the evidence is and how stupid it may seem rationally, he will not consider any alternative to materialistic atheism. Now, who is peddling myths and behaving as a "fundamentalist obscurantist?" Who is holding back "the search for truth?" Who is the "dogmatic philosopher ignoring the evidence?"

Instead of accepting such foolishness, we should follow the rational logic of Nobel Prize winner and physicist Arthur Compton who said:

> For myself, faith begins with the realization that a supreme intelligence brought the universe into being and created man. It is not difficult for me to have this faith, for it is incontrovertible that where there is a plan there is intelligence - an orderly, unfolding universe testifies to the truth of the most majestic statement ever uttered - "In the beginning God."[51]

Nobel Physics Laureate, Arno Penzias summed up the dilemma for atheists:

> Astronomy leads us to a unique event, a universe which was created out of nothing and delicately balanced to provide exactly the conditions required to support life. In the absence of an absurdly improbable accident, the observations of modern science seem to suggest an underlying, one might say, supernatural plan.[52]

Like Anthony Flew, other former atheists have been forced to admit their error when they come up against the logic of the design argument. Professor of Mathematical Physics Frank Tipler wrote:

> When I began my career as a cosmologist some twenty years ago, I was a convinced atheist. I never in my wildest dreams imagined that one day I would be writing a book purporting to show that the central claims of Judeo-Christian theology are in fact true, that these claims are straightforward deductions of the laws of physics as we now understand them. I have been forced into these conclusions by the inexorable logic of my own special branch of physics.[53]

The real reason many atheists resist acknowledging intelligent design is because if they accept the fact that there is design in the universe, then they know this design could not be the work of evolved intelligence. Instead, it must be the product of a transcendent intelligence and the options for this in "Who's Who?" are restricted, with God as the leading suspect. As George MacDonald the Scottish writer puts it: "to give truth to him who does not love the truth is only to give more reasons for misinterpretation." Or to put it another way, atheistic evolution is a fairy tale for grown-ups!

IN THE ABSENCE OF ANY OTHER PROOF, the thumb alone would convince me of God's existence.

Sir Isaac Newton, mathematician

MORALITY ARGUMENT:
WHAT EXACTLY IS YOUR QUESTION?

LIBERTY CANNOT BE ESTABLISHED without morality, nor morality without faith.
Alexis de Tocqueville, French political thinker and historian

Popular author and speaker, Ravi Zacharias was speaking at a forum on a university campus and he recounts the following challenge:

"Ah," a sceptical student questioned, "Is there not too much evil in the world to be a God?"

"But, surely," said Zacharias, "when you use the term 'evil' you are pre-supposing good and if there is objective good then there must be a moral law to reflect this. But when you admit there is a moral law, then you must admit a moral law giver – but then that's what you are trying to disprove and not prove! So, if there is no law giver, then there is no good or evil – so what is your meaningless question?"[54]

This encounter demonstrates a major difficulty for atheism. If there is no God, then there can be no objective good or bad moral values. There can only be our subjective views as we have no standard to determine good or bad with. Morals standards do not just appear from nothing. If they did, then how can we logically ask people to follow them? Leading atheist Prof. Richard Dawkins in writing a published letter to his 10 year old daughter advised that "next time somebody tells you that something is true, why not say to them: 'what kind of evidence is there for that?'"[55]

So, Prof. Dawkins what kind of objective evidence have you got that your daughter should follow your moral parental advice? If all morality is relative, then all moral judgments are equally valid. So, how can we consistently condemn evils such as: child abuse, Hitler murdering 6 million Jews or 9/11? Surely, if killing Jews is consistent with Hitler's moral framework then moral relativists must accept that his framework is as justified as theirs.

Indeed, at the Nuremberg trials the sole surviving senior Nazi on trial, Hermann Göring claimed that the Nazis were not guilty of any crime because their laws allowed the persecution of the Jews. Göring recognised that moral relativism would get him off the hook. Interestingly, Chief U.S. Prosecutor, Justice Robert Jackson, disagreed[56] and described the Nazi regime as morally as well as legally wrong and that they had violated "the moral sense of mankind."

If there truly is no God, then we should drop words that are inherent to our lives like: "ought not/ought to," "should not/should do," "responsible" "must/must not" from our laws, newspapers, codes of conduct and relationships as what right have we to impose obligations on others? Also, it would be impossible to logically criticise war, oppression, and crime or alternatively to praise, love or promote human rights. For how can we say something is absolutely wrong if we don't know what is absolutely right?

If there are no absolute morals, can child abuse ever be morally neutral or even good? Is choosing to engage in racism, slavery, and torture really no different to a preference for strawberry instead of chocolate ice cream? Yes, morals can be taught as well as innate but does that negate their objectivity – does teaching mathematics make it subjective?

On the contrary, we are all conscious of a moral faculty in our minds that gives rise to a "moral experience." I have never met anyone yet, who from their earliest recollection does not remember the probing of the conscience about what they "ought" to do when arriving at a potential moral conflict. As C.S. Lewis puts it:

> Human beings all over the earth, have this curious idea that they ought to behave in a certain way, and cannot really get rid of it. Secondly, that they do not in fact behave that way. They know the Law of Nature; they break it. These two facts are the foundation of all clear thinking about ourselves and the universe we live in.[57]

It is true that not all moral codes in every corner of this earth are the same in every aspect but there is a commonality of "core values." For instance, respect for parents and elders is universally admired whereas disrespect has never been admired. To quote Lewis again:

> Think of a country where people were admired for running away in battle, or where a man felt proud of double-crossing all the people who had been kindest to him. You might just as well try to imagine a country where two and two made five. Men have differed as regards what people you ought to be unselfish to - whether it was only your own family, or your fellow countrymen, or everyone. But they have always agreed that you ought not to put yourself first. Selfishness has never been admired. Men have

differed as to whether you should have one wife or four. But they
have always agreed that you must not simply have any woman
you liked.[58]

If there are no objective truths (and morals are truths), then why
bother studying, researching or seeking to discover new information
about the universe. Can two plus two sometimes not equal four? I have
never met an atheist yet who is willing to jump out a window at the top
of a tower block to demonstrate that the Law of Gravity is just a subjective truth! Should we be open-minded about a car speeding towards us
as we cross the road?

Moral relativists in fact actually get themselves into a philosophical
twist. If relativity were really true, then it follows there must be something to which all things are relative, but which is not relative itself. In
simple terms, something must be absolute before we can understand
that everything is relative to it.

Norman Geisler tells an amusing story of a student who was a strong
advocate of moral relativism:

> One student, an atheist, wrote a paper on the topic of moral
> relativism. He argued, "All morals are relative; there is no abso-
> lute standard of justice or rightness; it's all a matter of opinion;
> you like chocolate, I like vanilla," and so on. His paper provided
> both his reasons and his documentation. It was the right length,
> on time, and stylishly presented in a handsome blue folder.
>
> After the professor read the entire paper, he wrote on the front
> cover, "F, I don't like blue folders!" When the student got the
> paper back he was enraged. He stormed into the professor's
> office and protested,
>
> " 'F! I don't like blue folders!' That's not fair! That's not right!
> That's not just!"
>
> Raising his hand to quiet the bombastic student, the professor
> calmly retorted, "Wait a minute. Hold on. I read a lot of papers.
> Let me see....wasn't your paper the one that said there is no such
> thing as fairness, rightness, and justice?"
>
> "Yes," the student answered.
>
> "Fine, then," the professor responded. "I don't like blue. You get
> an F!"

Suddenly the lightbulb went on in the student's head. He realized he really did believe in moral absolutes. He at least believed in justice.[59]

Moral relativists self-defeat themselves when they claim:

1. "All truth is relative" – are you relatively sure?
2. "There is no such thing as truth" – is this statement the truth then?
3. "There is no such thing as absolutes" – are you absolutely sure?
4. "All truths are meaningless" – is your statement meaningless then?
5. "Never say never" – you just did!
6. "What is true for you is true for you" – so, I can never be wrong?
7. "You should be tolerant of all religious beliefs"—do you tolerate my religious intolerance belief of pluralism?
8. "You should not judge" – are you judging me?

No atheist has ever explained how an impersonal, amoral initial cause through a random amoral process has produced a moral basis for human life, while at the same time denying any objective moral basis for good or evil. As Dave Hunt reminded us: "There are no morals in nature. Try to find a compassionate crow or an honest eagle – or a sympathetic hurricane."[60]

Atheist Oxford Professor, Richard Dawkins accepts the moral relativist consequences of atheism and adds:

The universe we observe has precisely the properties we should expect if there is at the bottom, no design, no purpose, no evil and no other good. Nothing but blind, pitiless indifference. DNA neither knows nor cares. DNA just is. And we dance to its music.

Leaving aside how in a world, as described above, Dawkins can deduce what "design, purpose, evil and good" is, why do we care and why do we know then? Do computers know each other? Do computers sympathise with each other? Maybe Dawkins would like to tell the victims of Hitler that he was just dancing to his DNA! What kind of criminal justice system would we have if courts were told that criminals just danced to their DNA? Why has the Western world just fought a war with Bin Laden if he was just dancing to his DNA?

Ironically, Dawkins wrote to a British Newspaper[61] protesting that it was "morally repugnant" for a UK Government Department to conduct experiments on apes. Obviously, his DNA cares about such things. Dawkins in another classic example of hypocrisy derides creationists as "intolerant" and states that he and his atheistic colleagues "despise"[62] them—tolerance obviously does not apply to Christians whose "DNA just is!"

Conclusion

We are all instinctively aware that absolute truths and moral values exist and, indeed, conduct our lives on that premise. Even the person who denies that absolute values exist, values their right to state this.

A student of mine once told me there were no absolute values. I asked him in what context would he say it was permissible to kill a healthy new born baby? He replied that if the world population was too great then that would be a valid reason. I then asked him what his reaction would be if the class decided that the baby should live and he should die simply because they did not like the colour of his coat. He replied that this would be unfair as that was not a valid justification for making such a decision. I then simply pointed out to him that his moral relativism was self-defeating as he had just demonstrated by his words that he clearly believed in the absolute moral position of justice and fairness.

G.K. Chesterton summed up other inconsistencies of atheists:

> For all denunciation implies a moral doctrine of some kind; and the modern revolutionist doubts not only the institution he denounces, but the doctrine by which he denounces it. Thus he writes one book complaining that imperial oppression insults the purity of women, and then he writes another book in which he insults it himself. As a politician, he will cry out that war is a waste of life, and then, as a philosopher, that all life is waste of time. A Russian pessimist will denounce a policeman for killing a peasant, and then prove by the highest philosophical principles that the peasant ought to have killed himself. A man denounces marriage as a lie, and then denounces aristocratic profligates for treating it as a lie. The man of this school goes first to a political meeting, where he complains that savages are treated as if they were beasts; then he takes his hat and umbrella and goes on to a

scientific meeting, where he proves that they practically are beasts. In short, the modern revolutionist, being an infinite sceptic, is always engaged in undermining his own mines. In his book on politics he attacks men for trampling on morality; in his book on ethics he attacks morality for trampling on men. Therefore the modern man in revolt has become practically useless for all purposes of revolt. By rebelling against everything he has lost his right to rebel against anything.[63]

Atheists all want absolute truths when it suits them. They want their doctors, politicians, medicine labels, and spouses to be absolutely true with them. They definitely want them to be morally obliged to tell the truth! As Augustine put it: "We love truth when it enlightens us but we hate it when it convicts us."

It is said of the atheist Voltaire that when he had atheist friends over for dinner they boasted openly, while being served, of their atheism. However, Voltaire told them to keep quiet, as he didn't want such unbelief in front of the hired help because if they believed this they might murder him in his sleep and rob him. If, we don't have absolute morality, then we have to accept the consequences of this. Atheistic Princeton professor Peter Singer openly advocates infanticide of disabled newborn children and states:

> Human babies are not born self-aware, or capable of grasping that they exist over time. They are not persons . . . . The life of a newborn is of less value than the life of a pig, a dog, or a chimpanzee.[64]

Ironically Singer is reported[65] as spending his own money to look his mother who is suffering from Alzheimers disease – one wonders why he thinks she is any more a person than a disabled child? Richard Dawkins also openly states his support for eugenics:

> If you can breed cattle for milk yield, horses for running speed, and dogs for herding skill, why on Earth should it be impossible to breed humans for mathematical, musical or athletic ability?[66]

Speaking of the mentally disabled, another atheist goes further:

> What are we to say about them? The natural conclusion....would be that their status is that of mere animals. And perhaps we should go on to conclude that they may be used as non-human animals are used – perhaps as laboratory subjects, or as food.[67]

Convicted mass murderer Jeffrey Dahmer before his death stated:

> If a person doesn't think that there is a God to be accountable
> to, then what's the point of trying to modify your behaviour to
> keep it within acceptable ranges? That's how I thought anyway.
> I always believed the theory of evolution as truth, that we all just
> came from the slime. When we died, you know, that was it, there
> is nothing, and I've since come to believe that the Lord Jesus
> Christ is truly God, and I believe that I, as well as everyone else,
> will be accountable to Him.[68]

One atheist has even published an academic book arguing that rape
is simply a by-product of evolved differences between the sexualities of
males and females or an adaptation. When challenged on what grounds
he personally felt rape was wrong he admitted he had no absolute
standard for judging as it[69] was simply was his own opinion.

James Watson, the Nobel Prize winning discoverer of DNA and the
first director of the Human Genome Project, also promotes eugenics
and in his polemic at a conference at UCLA in 1998 stated:

> I think it's complete nonsense ... saying we're sacred and should
> not be changed…to say we've got a perfect genome and there's
> some sanctity? I'd like to know where that idea comes from
> because it's utter silliness.

However, he admitted the reason why he felt at liberty to advocate
such a view was the absence of an objective source of absolute morality:
"If we could make better human beings by knowing how to add genes,
why shouldn't we do it? What's wrong with it? Who is telling us not to
[do] it?"[70]

Atheists need to make their choice: either God exists and there is an
absolute standard of morality or He does not and as Fyodor Dostoevsky
said everything is permitted.

Vanity of vanities, saith the Preacher, vanity of vanities; all is vanity.

What profit hath a man of all his labour which he taketh under the sun?

*One generation passeth away, and another generation cometh: but the earth abideth
for ever*

The sun also ariseth, and the sun goeth down, and hasteth to his place where he arose.

The wind goeth toward the south, and turneth about unto the north; it whirleth about continually, and the wind returneth again according to his circuits.

All the rivers run into the sea; yet the sea is not full; unto the place from whence the rivers come, thither they return again.

All things are full of labour; man cannot utter it: the eye is not satisfied with seeing, nor the ear filled with hearing.

The thing that hath been, it is that which shall be; and that which is done is that which shall be done: and there is no new thing under the sun.

Ecclesiastes 1:2-9

THINKING ATOMS DISCUSSING MORALITY IS ABSURD.
Ravi Zacharias, Christian apologeticist

WITHOUT GOD, EVERYTHING IS PERMITTED.
Fyodor Dostoevsky, Russian novelist

"HOW CAN THOSE WHO SCORN GOD REVERE MEN?"
Sun Tzu, Ancient Chinese author

IF I WERE ASKED TODAY THE MAIN CAUSE of the ruinous Revolution that has swallowed up some sixty million of our people, I could not put it more accurately than to repeat: 'Men have forgotten God; that's why all this has happened.'
Alexander Solzhenitsyn, dissident Soviet authoer

IT IS WHEN PEOPLE FORGET GOD THAT TYRANTS FORGE THEIR CHAINS.
Patrick Henry, prominent American Revolutionist

CONSCIOUSNESS ARGUMENT: TO BE OR NOT TO BE?

I AGREE THAT ONE OF THE GREATEST RISKS of this focus on the genome . . . is that we overstate its significance and that we draw the conclusion that everything about us -- from what we had for breakfast this morning to who we chose as our life's partner -- is something that's hard-wired into our DNA, and free will goes out the window, and we move into this mind-set of genetic determinism. The scientific basis for that does not exist.

Dr. Francis Collins, Head of the Human Genome Project

An atheistic student, Chang stated in an English Major class of mine: "the only thing I believe in is chemicals." I pointed out to him that: as his statement of belief in materialism was not made of molecular "chemicals" so his belief was self-defeating and illogical. He had failed his own test! It would be like me saying: "I cannot speak English" – when I have just proven by my statement that I can.

However, to prove beyond a shadow of a doubt his error I offered him the chance to test his hypothesis. The challenge I gave him was to go with me to the local mortuary and there choose one dead body of "chemicals" and I would allow him to use any chemical to make that recently dead person live again. After all, I reasoned with him, this should be easy to an intelligent scientifically trained young man as "chance" managed to bring this "chemical consciousness" to over six billion people. Despite also offering him the chance to utilise the services of any skilled doctor or scientist, he unsurprisingly declined to test his theory!

Why? You don't need a PhD from Harvard to know that the human body has a conscious soul that is different from its materiality. If our emotions are material, can you weigh your "thoughts" or bottle "love" or "envy" and sell these "chemicals" at your local Wal-Mart? Are chemicals to be held responsible for people falling in love? Even Einstein confessed: "Gravitation is not responsible for people falling in love."

One of the great absurdities of the atheistic worldview of consciousness is that if they believe the brain is the product of irrational, unguided mechanisms then how can they trust it to be correct? How can they trust their power of reasoning that creationism is wrong and atheism is the best interpretation? It maybe that their brains haven't fully evolved yet to the level of creationists in order to comprehend the evidence for creationism! If atheism is true, then we have no way of knowing anything is true as chemicals do not rationalise they just react. Just think, would you trust a surgeon to operate on you who told you his surgical procedures were blindly governed by "random movements of chemicals?"

Atheistic Biologist, Richard Dawkins said that anyone who denied evolution was "ignorant, stupid or insane (or wicked, but I'd rather not consider that)."[71] Which raises the question – if our thinking and morality is simply a by-product of accidental chemical reactions, why is Prof. Dawkins so confident he can rationally identify ignorance, stupidity and wickedness?

As far as we can comprehend, the world has a rational structure, which mirrors the rationality of the human mind. If the world evolved by chance it would be highly unlikely that human experience would replicate the reality of the world the way we conclude it does. Theologian, Prof. John Frame explains:

> The hypothesis of absolute personality to explain the formation of the universe explains the data far better than the hypothesis of ultimate impersonality. An absolute personality can make a rational universe and his plan for creation and providence is therefore rational. The absolute personality is able to make man in His image and to equip him to understand the universe as much as he needs to. Why should we prefer a hypothesis of ultimate impersonality when that creates such an enormous gap between the nature of the Creator (non-rational) and the nature of the universe including human beings (rational)?[72]

Our ability to rationalise can only come from either a pre-existing intelligence or from pure atomic matter. However, no atheist has ever explained how you can get something completely different in the form of conscious thinking, feeling, believing, purposeful and worshipping creatures from atomic matter that does not possess any of these qualities. That's truly getting something from nothing! Some "clever" atheists have even suggested that consciousness is a "by-product of biological processes," not realising that they are now implicitly adding "spooky" and "spiritual mental powers" to what they maintain is "pure atomic matter!"

Theologian and philosopher, Prof. J.P. Moreland summed up the difficulty for atheism in explaining how you get from molecular atoms to living consciousness:

If you start with particles, you may end up with a more complicated arrangement of particles, but you are still going to have particles. You are not going to have minds or consciousness.

However, if you begin with an infinite mind, then you can explain how finite minds could come into existence. What doesn't make sense – and many atheistic evolutionists are conceding – is the idea of getting a mind to squirt into existence by starting with brute, dead, mindless matter. That's why some of them are trying to get rid of consciousness by saying it is not real and that we are just computers. However, that's a pretty difficult position to maintain while you are conscious![73]

Conclusion

Some sceptics try to deny that there is any logic in the world and that there is nothing that is truly "knowable." This was the view popularised by influential philosopher, Immanuel Kant who maintained that, "you can't know anything about the real world." The fatal flaw in this position, which Kant never explained, is how does he know what the "real world" is then? Also, his claim is self-defeating, as by claiming you cannot know anything about the real world; Kant claimed to know that the real world is unknowable! This reminds me of the story of student who asked his philosophy professor: "how do I know that I exist?" The learned professor looked down from his notes and fixed his eyes at the young man and replied, "And whom shall I say is asking?"

Deep down in our sub-conscience we all have a vacuum that only God can fill. Atheism has no answer to this fact. In 1999, Religion Today reported that even children who had not been exposed to organised religion manifest this:

Children believe in God regardless of whether they are exposed to religious faith, a study found. Oxford University psychologist Olivera Petrovitch and her research assistants found that children they studied in Britain and Japan gave similar answers when asked who created various natural objects, she reported in the magazine Science & Spirit. The children, who had not been influenced by concepts of God from organized religions, had abstract notions of a creator. Petrovitch's researchers in Japan said they were surprised at the children's responses. "My Japanese research assistants kept telling me, We Japanese don't think about God as creator - it's just not part of Japanese philosophy," she said.[74]

The ultimate irony of this book is that any one reading it, whether atheist or not, has conceded the argument merely by studying it in a logical and rational manner. In order to review this evidence as a real exercise in truth finding, and not merely a chance encounter between bundles of genetic matter, the reader assumes: that the universe is coherent, consistent, and orderly; that there is genuine rational thought (and communication of ideas) and that truth, design, predictability and natural law actually govern the processes of the universe.

Put simply, the reader has assumed a theistic worldview (despite not acknowledging it) that God exists, created mankind, and created the world in which we find ourselves. For, to say the universe is not designed, atheists must know what design is. To say theism is not true, atheists must know what is true and so on. This would be like using the laws of science to prove that the laws of science cannot be trusted.

C.S. Lewis summed up atheistic circular reasoning:

> A theory which explained everything else in the whole universe but which made it impossible to believe that our thinking was valid, would be utterly out of court. For that theory would itself have been reached by thinking, and if thinking is not valid that theory would, of course, be itself demolished. It would have destroyed its own credentials. It would be an argument, which proved that no argument was sound-proof that there are no such things as proofs - which is nonsense.[75]

Who hath measured the waters in the hollow of his hand, and meted out heaven with the span, and comprehended the dust of the earth in a measure, and weighed the mountains in scales, and the hills in a balance?

Who hath directed the Spirit of the LORD, or being his counsellor hath taught him? With whom took he counsel, and who instructed him, and taught him in the path of judgment, and taught him knowledge, and shewed to him the way of understanding?

Behold, the nations are as a drop of a bucket, and are counted as the small dust of the balance: behold, he taketh up the isles as a very little thing.

And Lebanon is not sufficient to burn, nor the beasts thereof sufficient for a burnt offering.

All nations before him are as nothing; and they are counted to him less than nothing, and vanity. To whom then will ye liken God? or what likeness will ye compare unto him? The workman melteth a graven image, and the goldsmith spreadeth it over with gold, and casteth silver chains.

He that is so impoverished that he hath no oblation chooseth a tree that will not rot; he seeketh unto him a cunning workman to prepare a graven image, that shall not be moved.

Have ye not known? have ye not heard? hath it not been told you from the beginning? have ye not understood from the foundations of the earth?
It is he that sitteth upon the circle of the earth, and the inhabitants thereof are as grasshoppers; that stretcheth out the heavens as a curtain, and spreadeth them out as a tent to dwell in: That bringeth the princes to nothing; he maketh the judges of the earth as vanity.

Yea, they shall not be planted; yea, they shall not be sown: yea, their stock shall not take root in the earth: and he shall also blow upon them, and they shall wither, and the whirlwind shall take them away as stubble.

To whom then will ye liken me, or shall I be equal? saith the Holy One.

Isaiah 40:12-25

CONSCIOUSNESS IS EITHER INEXPLICABLE ILLUSION, OR ELSE REVELATION.
C.S. Lewis

THE SOUL OF MAN IS IMMORTAL AND IMPERISHABLE.
Plato

MEANING OF LIFE ARGUMENT: A HERO OR A FOOL?

> IF THE WHOLE UNIVERSE HAS NO MEANING, we should never have found out that it has no meaning: just as, if there were no light in the universe and therefore no creatures with eyes, we should never know it was dark. Dark would be without meaning.
> C.S. Lewis

In China in March 2005, 100,000 people attended the funeral for a schoolteacher Yin Xuemei who died from injuries from being hit by a car after pushing her pupils out of the way in order to save them.[76] I questioned an atheistic Chinese student who visited me, "If there is no God and no life after death, then why do the Chinese people think this teacher did something the newspapers say was an "heroic" act and which we "should learn from?" Surely, she did the stupidest thing in the world for her and her family? Should she not have saved herself first, even if it meant the children died? Is it not foolish to die for others and to give up her brief chance of the only life she will ever have? He admitted there was no rational atheistic answer.

For, if there is no God, then the evil of men goes unpunished and the good done in the world un-rewarded. Why be generous? Why be faithful to your wife and family? Why be loyal to your country? Why not be the most selfish person you can be? Stalin, Hitler and Pol Pot murdered millions, yet none of them ever faced a court of law for their crimes – did they literally get away with murder? It certainly is a bit tough on atheists like Karl Marx who at the end of his life stated: "I have sacrificed my whole fortune to the revolutionary struggle."[77]

Most atheists live inconsistently to their beliefs and instinctively praise heroic acts like that of Yin Xuemei. This is because, in all cultures and religions of the world people have an intuitive understanding that there is more to life than our transient presence on earth. We are all conscious deep in our hearts of an afterlife with a "day of reckoning" to follow. Even if we were to accept that such altruistic traits "accidentally evolved" surely they would have died out by now as mankind strives for the "survival of the fittest." Yet, here we are 150,000 years after evolutionists tell us man first inhabited this earth, and benevolence is still with us. As one writer explains:

> The prevalence of altruistic acts—providing benefits to a recipient
> at a cost to the donor—can seem hard to reconcile with the idea
> of the selfish gene, the notion that evolution at its base acts solely
> to promote genes that are most adept at engineering their own
> proliferation.[78]

This final heading could be summarized as the search for the answer why is there something rather than nothing? Or, why is there an "is"?

If there is no God, then both mankind and this universe are inevitably doomed so life has no purpose or meaning for a universe cannot generate its own meaning or value. This universe, as we saw in our review of the Second Law of Thermodynamics, is running out of useable energy and will one day burn out and all matter will collapse into black holes. Mankind is therefore slowly dying so we are like prisoners on death row just awaiting the execution call. Has our life really no purpose or ultimate significance? This reminds me of a story from N. Ireland that is told of an atheist who had just died and one mourner quipped at his funeral wake when looking into his casket "There is Johnny – all dressed up and nowhere to go."

Clarence Darrow was a renowned criminal lawyer and atheist who once famously defended John T. Scopes, a teacher accused of teaching the evolutionary origin of man, rather than the doctrine of divine creation. At the end of his life he confessed:

> My colleagues say that I am a success. Many honours have come
> my way, but in the Bible is a sentence, which expresses the way I
> feel about my life. That sentence is this: "We have toiled all night
> and taken nothing."[79]

Ironically, atheists think that if they could get rid of God, they can live free from the shackles that bind them. Instead, they discover that by removing God, they remove the only meaning for their life. Paradoxically, often the most ardent atheists are keen to push what they regard are meaningful agendas and are extreme feminist, environmentalist, homosexual and animal rights lobbyists. If there is no meaning in life and no future for this planet, why do they care so much?

Richard Dawkins tries an inconsistent explanation. He maintains that while he is an atheistic Darwinian as a scientist (meaning that our brain is a product of purposeless chance) he is passionately anti-Darwinian when it comes to how we should conduct our human affairs.[80] Talk about trying to have your cake and eating it! He claims our "brains can thwart Darwinian designs." In other words, he is arguing that the creature has somehow (no explanation is offered how) evolved to usurp his creator. Another person once foolishly believed he could do the same: "I will ascend above the heights of the clouds; I will be like the most High."[81]

Another problem for atheism is that if there is no God and all our thoughts, desires, actions are just random chemical processes in our brain governed by the fixed laws of nature then there is NO FREE WILL! For if man is a totally material entity, then any apparent freedom is illusory as the "fixed laws of nature" govern our actions. The Oxford University chemist and prominent atheist, Peter Atkins said as much: "Free will is merely the ability to decide, and the ability to decide is nothing other than the organized interplay of shifts of atoms."[82]

So, why do we even waste time trying to punish criminals if their behaviour is fixed by the environment or genetics? Why do we make a distinction in law from crimes committed with full mental faculties and those done by insane persons? Why do we blame ourselves and feel guilty when we make a bad choice? Richard Dawkins when confronted in 2006 with the problematic question of freewill on a radio debate tried to avoid the problem:

> I'm not interested in free will what I am interested in is the ridiculous suggestion that if science can't say where the origin of matter comes from theology can. The origin of matter... the origin of the whole universe, is a very, very difficult question. It's one that scientists are working on. It's one that they hope eventually to solve. Just as before Darwin, biology was a mystery. Darwin solved that. Now cosmology is a mystery. The origin of the universe is a mystery; it's a mystery to everyone. Physicists are working on it. They have theories.[83]

Atheism simply says we are no different from plants or animals? But, what plant or animal manufactures high-tech products, practices hobbies, solves mathematics problems, enjoys art, laughs at jokes, thinks abstractly, obeys a conscience and worships a higher being? What animal has a complex vocabulary, uses written symbols, observes laws of grammar, and thinks up rhymes and poetry? By way of aside, no atheist has ever come up with a credible reason how, if the man has been on earth for more than 155,000 years, it took man 150,000 years to learn to communicate in written form as the oldest known language is only just over 5,000 years. After all, a two year old child can write the alphabet!

Conclusion

The ultimate irony here is that atheists aggressively try to "convert" theists to their "atheistic religious system" when they presumably know better than any of us that we are "fated to believe" our theism because of our chemical make-up, irrespective of the persuasiveness of their arguments. Perhaps, they would do better to shake us or inject us with another chemical so that the arrangement of molecules in our brains would make us atheists. But, no – they argue with us! Why?

A letter was sent to the editor of The Daily Courier (Forest City, North Carolina, USA), September 22, 2001.[84] It sums up the total inadequacy of atheism to reflect any meaning on life:

> To the editor:
> I'm in my 30's but I've lived long enough to see a lot of pain and senseless tragedy in life. A prime example has been the recent terrorist attacks in New York and Washington, D.C.
> As I try to come to grips with the catastrophe, I am beginning to question the worldview I acquired while attending public school. I am not finding reasonable answers to four questions that have come to the forefront of my mind since terrorists brutally attacked our country.
> My first question pertains to human dignity and worth. Why do human beings have worth, and where did they get it? Our nation is outraged at the senseless deaths of thousands of Americans, but what is it that makes us lament the loss? My textbooks explained that the appearance of life in the universe came about by time and chance, which in turn changed single-cell organisms into complex human beings. According to Darwin's theory of Evolution, the strongest survive, those that can adapt will do so, and the rest are replaced by the fittest. If the origin of human life is the result of a chance mutation in the last several billion years, where does

human worth come from? Scientifically, the World Trade victims lost out in the struggle for survival, end of story. Why does my heart still grieve for the dead and their families?

My second question has to do with right and wrong. Why do I put the question of pain and evil in a moral context? Why do I react so strongly against these attacks on our nation, and denounce the acts as immoral and wrong? Of course I could say that I didn't like the terrorism, but how can I say that it is wrong? Any time that I denounce something, I am implying a moral law of some sort by which to know the difference between good and bad. But we've all been taught that there is no unchanging reference point by which to differentiate between right and wrong. It was an unquestioned assumption in all of my science classes that nothing exists except natural phenomena.

Madalyn Murray O'Hair said it succinctly when she wrote, "There are no supernatural forces, no supernatural entities such as gods, or heavens, or hells, or life after death." I assume that the terrorists who hijacked our planes were willing to give up their lives for Allah's cause, and that they sincerely felt that their actions were good and worthy. Yet we consider their actions to be both vile and immoral. On what basis do I denounce their deeds as evil if there is no higher power above both these people and the Americans?

My third question has to do with justice. I hope that justice can be brought swiftly upon the perpetrators of this crime, but it might take a long time. There is the possibility that I will not see full justice brought to this situation during my lifetime. Sometimes I am actually attracted to the idea of a final judgment of the living and the dead that some people talk about. There are a lot of things that I've seen in life which I hope someday will be put right, but I cannot imagine how this could happen in a universe where nothing but natural phenomena exists.

My fourth question pertains to this sudden interest in prayer. I seem to be getting contradictory messages. Who is the god that everyone is praying to all of sudden? Prayer has been banned from public schools for three decades and now we are having a National Day of Prayer. Has our government decided that there really is some higher power after all? If so, is it watching from a distance, or does it really care about those who died? Is it a vague force or does it have personality?

I am questioning the assumptions of materialism and naturalism because they are not comforting me in my time of need. If I must accept the reality of evil and suffering, can I ever hope to find a cause and a purpose in it?

The following words from respected British evolutionist and author Richard Dawkins only serve to shake my confidence in finding satisfying answers in naturalism. Mr Dawkins speaks about the logical conclusions of this world view in a book called River Out of Eden, saying, "In a universe of blind physical forces and genetic replication, some people are going to get hurt, other people are going to get lucky, and you won't find any rhyme or reason in it, nor any justice. The universe we observe has precisely the properties we should expect if there is, at bottom, no design, no purpose, no evil and no other good. Nothing but blind, pitiless indifference. DNA neither knows nor cares. DNA just is. And we dance to its music."

Bradley Mast
Mooresboro, NC

 THE VERDICT

The acknowledged media champion of contemporary atheism is Prof. Richard Dawkins of Oxford University and for that reason, if nothing else, we have quoted from him extensively in this study. Dawkins boasts that, "Darwin made it possible to be an intellectually fulfilled atheist." [85] Frankly, that says more about the limited intellectual ambition of Richard Dawkins than anything else. Let us not so quickly surrender our critical reasoning ability.

In researching for this book, I undertook to read the writings of all the famed writers of atheism such as Dawkins, Russell, Flew and Atkins. What surprised me most, was not just the lack of logic to their arguments but also the lack of any substantive argument at all. The best they could cumulatively offer was "just because nothing has not produced something before should not necessarily infer that it is impossible." Or in reference to the Second Law of Thermodynamics some argue, "there is an exception to every law" – to which theists can simply reply how do you know that the law that says, "there is an exception to every law" does not have an exception?

Science has improved our understanding of life but it cannot account for everything. As William Lane Craig cited in his debate[86] with atheist Peter Atkins, science cannot explain:

1. Mathematics and logic (science cannot prove them because it pre-supposes them),
2. Metaphysical truths (such as, there are minds that exist other than my own),
3. Ethical judgments (you can't prove by science that the Nazis were evil, because morality is not subject to the scientific method),
4. Aesthetic judgments (the beautiful, like the good, cannot be scientifically proven)
5. And, ironically Science itself - the belief that the scientific method (i.e. searching for causes by observation and repetition) discovers truth can't be proven by the scientific method itself. Science itself is simply a product of the mind.

If science cannot explain all of the above, the way is surely open for alternative explanations with religion being the leading candidate to fill the vacuum. Christianity, especially, can provide meaningful answers to these most fundamental questions. To all reasonable people, this would seem an eminently sensible approach.

If I were instructed by a client with a litigation brief to argue that God does not exist against the overwhelming cumulative evidence that demonstrates that He does, I would advise my clients to settle out of court or drop it immediately! No honest lawyer in his right mind would advise otherwise. Yet, so many unsuspecting atheists are still trusting these phony lawyers that masquerade under the title "evolutionary scientist" or "atheistic philosopher" that they have a legitimate case. If God were put on trial for withholding evidence of His existence, no reasonable judge or jury on earth would convict Him! Many claim attributes about themselves but few are able to evidence them.

Muhammed Ali, the famous and charismatic boxer, was once on an airplane when he was asked by a stewardess to fasten his seatbelt during some turbulent weather, "Superman don't need no seatbelt," he boasted.

"Superman, don't need no airplane either," the stewardess quickly retorted. This Emperor clearly had no clothes!

The question of God's existence is something that very few people are indifferent about. Indeed, atheists often have the strongest emotions in a discussion concerning it which itself is suggestive. Journalist and Yale educated lawyer, Lee Strobel investigated the existence of God and concluded that if he were to embrace atheistic Darwinism and its underlying premise of naturalism he would have to believe that:

1. Nothing produces everything
2. Non-life produces life
3. Randomness produces fine-tuning
4. Chaos produces information
5. Unconsciousness produces consciousness
6. Non-reason produces reason[87]

Frankly, that is just too many coincidences for any rational person to accept. Yet, atheists look you in the eye and boast that they believe this foolishness. We can conclude from the five categories of evidence set out in these five chapters that the First Cause of the universe must be independent of it and have the following characteristics:

1. Be self-existent, immaterial, timeless and nonspatial – since the First Cause created all of these;
2. Be incredibly powerful and intelligent – to design and create such a precise and vast universe; and
3. Be personal – we know that the Creator is timeless as He is outside of time. Since timeless impersonal forces (such as mathematical entities) do not have freewill so they cannot choose to convert nothing into something – therefore, the First Cause must also be personal.

In fact, these characteristics sum up the Bible's description of God. Interestingly, this characterization of God in this way is a unique concept among early world religions.

Why with all this overwhelming evidence for the existence of God do men, especially educated men, refuse to acknowledge their Creator? Are they "educated beyond their intelligence?" To paraphrase C.S. Lewis, "through what strange process has these learned scientists gone in order to make themselves blind to what all rational and logical men except them can see?" The Bible puts it more directly:

> For the invisible things of him from the creation of the world are clearly seen, being understood by the things that are made, even his eternal power and Godhead; so that they are without excuse: Because that, when they knew God, they glorified him not as God, neither were thankful; but became vain in their imaginations, and their foolish heart was darkened. Professing themselves to be wise, they became fools,
> Romans 1:20-22

> Because ye have said, We have made a covenant with death, and with hell are we at agreement; when the overflowing scourge shall pass through, it shall not come unto us: for we have made lies our refuge, and under falsehood have we hid ourselves:
> Therefore thus saith the Lord GOD, Behold, I lay in Zion for a foundation a stone, a tried stone, a precious corner stone, a sure foundation: he that believeth shall not make haste.
> Isaiah 28:15-16

An atheist once scoffed, "If there is a God, may he prove himself by striking me dead right now." Nothing happened. "You see, there is no God." A wiser person commented, "You've only proved that He is a gracious God." Atheists often mistake the grace and patience of God for weakness. It is amusing to hear atheists scoff at the power of God and they cannot even look directly at the sun!

The number of known stars is approximately equal to the number of sand grains in the world. As logic tells us that the effect cannot be greater than the cause just imagine the power of God who simply spoke all of those planets into existence without drawing breath. Yes, God is merciful and longsuffering but He is also a just God and He warns: "He, that being often reproved hardeneth his neck, shall suddenly be destroyed, and that without remedy." Proverbs 29:1

If you still have your brains switched on at this point you can only conclude that the existence of God is inescapable. However, there are many kinds of gods in the world today and it is popular to advocate the pluralistic view that there are many gods or that there is one God with many ways to reach Him. To such an illogicality, God Himself challenges the pluralist: "To whom then will ye liken me, or shall I be equal? saith the Holy One. Produce your cause, saith the LORD; bring forth your strong reasons," Isaiah 40:25; 41:21

Let us turn now and see how the rivals for Jesus Christ and the Christian God match up.

> For the invisible things of him from the creation of the world are clearly seen, being understood by the things that are made, even his eternal power and Godhead; so that they are without excuse:
> Because that, when they knew God, they glorified him not as God, neither were thankful; but became vain in their imaginations, and their foolish heart was darkened.
> Professing themselves to be wise, they became fools,
> And changed the glory of the uncorruptible God into an image made like to corruptible man, and to birds, and fourfooted beasts, and creeping things.
> Wherefore God also gave them up to uncleanness through the lusts of their own hearts, to dishonour their own bodies between themselves:
> Who changed the truth of God into a lie, and worshipped and served the creature more than the Creator, who is blessed for ever. Amen.
> Romans 1:20-25

How do we know there is only one God? "Jesus saith unto him, "I am the way, the truth, and the life; no man cometh unto the Father, but by me." John 14:6

LAW OF NON-CONTRADICTION
Sceptic: All religious beliefs are true
Christian: I believe you are going to hell

I AM CONVINCED THAT HE (GOD) DOES NOT PLAY DICE.
Albert Einstein

THIS MOST BEAUTIFUL SYSTEM could only proceed from the dominion of an intelligent and powerful being.
Sir Isaac Newton

Part 2

HOW DO WE KNOW THERE IS ONLY ONE GOD?

WHAT KIND OF GOD DO WE WORSHIP?

MEN ARE NOT FLATTERED by being shown that there has been a difference of
purpose between the Almighty and them
Abraham Lincoln

A young man was cycling through the heat of India and after spotting
a cremation site he stopped to converse with the Hindu priest. He pointed
to the pile of ashes that represented the remains of the cremated corpse
and asked the priest where the dead person was now.

"Young man," the Hindu priest replied, "that is a question you will
be asking all your life and you will never find the answer." Disillusioned
the young man cycled on having thought that if a priest does not know
what hope had he of ever discovering the answer.

Years later in a hospital bed, the same disillusioned young man
was handed a Bible. Turning to John 14:19 he read, "Because I live,
ye shall live also." He had found the answer. After receiving Christ as
his Saviour, the young man called Ravi Zacharias became a theistic
apologist and author.

All religions do not point to God and are not the same. Indeed, all
religions do not agree that all religions are the same. At the core of every
religion is an exclusivity of defining how a man can or cannot have a
relationship with God. Anyone who believes that all religions are the
same is simply showing their ignorance of the teachings of world
religions. The U.K.'s Prince Charles typified this ignorance when he
declared in 1996 that if he became King in succession to his mother he
wanted to be known as: "Defender of Faith" rather than the exclusive
Christian title of: "Defender of the Faith." Even some secular journalists
noted the illogicality of this and one commented, "You cannot defend
all faiths – at least not at the same time – because each has beliefs that
renders those of the others false."[88]

In philosophy and the reality of life we have what is called the Law
of Non-Contradiction. This law simply says that contradictory claims
cannot both be true. For instance, if you ask my wife and I where I was
born and I told you that I was born in U.K. but my wife replied that I
was born in Singapore you would be confused. Now, you don't think at
this point that I was born in two places; just that one of us has made a

mistake or misunderstood your question. One thing you would be sure of and that is that my wife's reply and mine could not be both correct! This is because as the Law of Non-Contradiction says contradictory claims cannot both be true. In fact, anyone who tries to refute the Law of Non-Contradiction is actually affirming it by implying that it is wrong and his or her belief is right. The law of Non-Contradiction is both self-evident and unavoidable.

Applying the Law of Non-Contradiction to religion gives us interesting results. Firstly, we know that atheism and theism cannot both be true – either God exists or He does not. Also, it helps us to understand the difference between Christianity and other religions. Either God is a personal transcendent God as Christians say or He is the universe as Hindus say. Either Jesus is the Son of God, died and rose from the dead or he is just a prophet and did not as the Qur'an says. Either non-Christians are going to hell when they die or they are caught in an indefinite cycle of re-incarnation as Buddhists believe. The more you study world religions you realise they have many more contradictory beliefs then similar ones and differ widely on the fundamental doctrines of Faith.

Some people like to patronise Christians and say that Jesus was a good man who taught good things but He wasn't God. C.S. Lewis in Mere Christianity summed up the inconsistency of this:

> I am trying here to prevent anyone saying the really foolish thing that people often say about Him: "I'm ready to accept Jesus as a great moral teacher, but I don't accept His claim to be God." That is one thing we must not say. A man who was merely a man and said the sort of thing Jesus said would not be a great moral teacher. He would either be a lunatic, on a level with the man who says he is a poached egg, or else he would be the Devil of Hell. You must make your choice. Either this man was, and is, the Son of God: or else a madman or something worse. You can shut Him up for a fool, you can spit at Him and kill him as a demon or you can fall at his feet and call Him Lord and God. But let us not come with any patronising nonsense about His being a great human teacher. He has not left that open to us. He did not intend to.

Atheists like to portray Christianity as narrow-minded because of the exclusivity of the claims of Jesus Christ. Yet, they never realise that they are guilty of the same intolerance when they state as a fact that Christianity is true and atheism is correct.

A tale that is told illustrates the Law of Non-Contradiction to religion. A pompous liberal preacher was visiting in a conservative Church and met what he regarded was "old fashioned holy roller" woman there.

"Do you really believe that Jonah was swallowed by a whale?" the preacher questioned condescendingly.

"Of course," the lady replied and added, "Indeed, if my Bible said that Jonah swallowed the whale I would believe it."

"Could you tell us how a whale could swallow a living man?" smirked the preacher.

"I am not sure," the lady replied, " but, when I get to heaven I will ask Jonah how it happened."

"But," purred the liberal preacher, "what happens if you get to heaven and you find out that Jonah is not there?"

"Well then," she retorted back, "you can ask him."

The Law of Non-Contradiction demonstrates in a humourous way in this story that either the Bible is correct in its statement about the existence and salvation of Jonah or it is not.

We know from the cosmological and divine design (teleological) evidences of the universe that God must be infinite because He created all space, all time and all matter from nothing. Infinite simply means that He is self-existent, non-spatial, immaterial, timeless, personal, unimaginably powerful and supremely intelligent etc. In other words, there is nothing lacking in Him.

The fact that God is infinite impliedly rules out all pantheistic religions such as the New Age Movement, Hinduism and some forms of Buddhism that equate God to the universe as we have seen that universe is not infinite as it had a beginning and was designed by another cause.

This fact also disproves polytheistic religions (the belief that there are many gods) such as Mormonism, as there logically cannot be more than one omnipresent infinite being. Let me explain more simply: If there was more than one God (e.g. God "A" and God "B"), then to distinguish one from the other they must differ in some way. If God "A" is infinite then God "B" must be less than infinite (i.e. infinite minus something), as the definition of infinite means that God "A" lacks nothing. Therefore, if God "B" is less than infinite he is not God! Therefore, we can only logically conclude that there can only be one Infinite Being or God who is transcendent or outside all time, all space and all matter.

There is a push on today based on pragmatism to make us give up the exclusivity of Jesus Christ. Recently a Lipscomb University theologian told an interfaith gathering at the university, "The most basic Christian commitment … is that we say we believe in the Lordship of Jesus. But, if we claim that, how can a Muslim or Jew trust us, if we say Jesus is the Lord of all Lords?"[89]

Indeed, many invoke the eastern parable re-told by Lillian Quigley of several blind men all feeling different parts of an elephant's anatomy to demonstrate pluralism.

> The first blind man put out his hand and touched the side of the elephant. "How smooth! An elephant is like a wall." The second blind man put out his hand and touched the trunk of the elephant. "How round! An elephant is like a snake." The third blind man put out his hand and touched the tusk of the elephant. "How sharp! An elephant is like a spear." The fourth blind man put out his hand and touched the leg of the elephant. "How tall! An elephant is like a tree." The fifth blind man reached out his hand and touched the ear of the elephant. "How wide! An elephant is like a fan." The sixth blind man put out his hand and touched the tail of the elephant. "How thin! An elephant is like a rope." [90]

The problem for this parable is that the storyteller himself is not blind and understands they are all wrong so it is self-defeating. You cannot logically say "Each of us is blind," and then add, "but I'll describe what the world really looks like." This is a clear contradiction. It also presumes that Christians are blind to the teachings of other religions in our rejection of pluralism.

However, Christians reject other religions because of the fact that we are aware of their contradictory beliefs to those of Jesus Christ. We have the truth of God revealed to us through the person of Jesus Christ, the Bible and Creation. A better analogy is to ask a pluralist, "Aren't you glad your airplane pilot doesn't think there are many places apart from the runway to land your plane?"

It may make you the most popular person to argue for religious pluralism and get you on CNN or the NY Times Bestseller List but it is not the truth.

Part 3

HOW DO WE KNOW THE BIBLE IS THE WORD OF GOD?

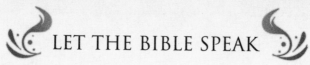

LET THE BIBLE SPEAK

THE BIBLE IS NO MERE BOOK, but a living creature, with a power that conquers all that oppose it.

Napoleon Bonaparte, Emporer of France

In 1947 a young shepherd boy, Muhammad adh-Dhib discovered in some caves North West of the Dead Sea near Jericho some jars containing some old leather scrolls. This accidental discovery was to have monumental significance for Bible scholars. What was found in the cave were 100 scrolls of the Old Testament some dating back as far as 200 BC. Until this discovery, the earliest extant copies of the Old Testament dated from 900 AD only. When analysed, it was discovered that the accuracy of the Old Testament text over this 1,000-year period was truly astonishing.

That God should have so wonderfully preserved His word should not surprise us for there is nothing ordinary about this book. The French philosopher Francois-Marie Arouet, who wrote under the pen-name of Voltaire, once boasted that the Bible would be extinct by 1850. After he died, his house and printing press on the French-Swiss border was taken over by the Swiss Bible Society. Obviously, he was not only a poor philosopher but also an even worse prophet!

The Bible has been more viciously attacked, ridiculed and blasphemed than any other book yet it reigns supreme as the world's best-selling book year on year. In 2002, the United Bible Societies reported[91] that more than 578,029,863 copies had been printed that year alone. Daniel Radosh of The New Yorker observed,

> The familiar observation that the Bible is the best-selling book of all time obscures a more startling fact: the Bible is the best-selling book of the year, every year. Calculating how many Bibles are sold in the United States is a virtually impossible task, but a conservative estimate is that in 2005 Americans purchased some twenty-five million Bibles—twice as many as the most recent Harry Potter book. The amount spent annually on Bibles has been put at more than half a billion dollars.[92]

Since 1450, more than 6.5 billion copies have been printed. The nearest rival is Mao Tse-Tung's Little Red Book which was sold or given away to around 900 million. The Bible had by the year 2002 been translated into more than 2,377 languages and no book has influenced the western world more than the Bible. Not bad for a book that was supposed to be extinct by 1850! The U.K.'s Times newspaper marvelled:

> Forget modern British novelists and TV tie-ins, the Bible is the best-selling book every year. If sales of the Bible were included in best-seller lists, it would be a rare week when anything else would achieve a look in. It is wonderful, weird ... that in this godless age... this one book should go on selling, every month.

The power of the Bible can even be seen in scientific advancement as 86% of Nobel Science prizes from 1901 through 1990 has been won by Jews and Protestants, with Jews taking 22% of the prizes. Protestants have taken two thirds (66%) of the Nobel Science prizes.[93] Although many of the prize winners were not religious, as John Hulley, a former senior economist with the World Bank in Washington, D.C., who is the author of the book, Comets, Jews, and Christians explains: "What we are talking about is the social environment. It is the religious people who create the environment and the secular who benefit from it. Fairness is in the backbone of both Jewish and Protestant cultures."[94]

The Bible was written under the inspiration of the Holy Spirit by over 40 different authors from many different walks of life including: shepherds, farmers, tent-makers, physicians, fishermen, priests, philosophers and kings. Despite these wide variations in background and the centuries it took to write it, the Bible is an extremely cohesive and unified book. The Bible has only one major theme: the progressive revelation of God through the person of His Son Jesus Christ. It identifies one problem, sin and it gives one answer, Jesus Christ.

Dr. Harry Ironside, who was a famous Bible preacher, in his younger days used to preach for the Salvation Army in the open air. One day as he was preaching in San Francisco, he noticed a man in the crowd writing on a card, which he presently handed to the speaker. The man was Arthur Lewis, a well-known atheist and lecturer. He proposed a challenge to the speaker to debate the subject, "Atheism versus Christianity," and offered to pay all expenses involved. Ironside read the card aloud to his audience and then said:

> "I accept on these conditions: First, that you promise to bring with you to the platform one man who was once an outcast, a

slave to sinful habits, but who heard you or some other infidel
lecture on atheism, was helped by it and cast away his sins and
became a new man and is today a respected member of society,
all because of your unbelief. Second, that you agree to bring with
you one woman who was once lost to all purity and goodness,
but who can now testify that atheism came to her while deep in
sin and implanted in her poor heart a hatred of impurity and a
love of holiness, causing her to become chaste and upright, all
through a disbelief in the Bible."

"Now, sir," he continued, "if you will agree, I promise to be there
with one hundred such men and women once just such lost souls,
who heard the gospel of the grace of God, believed it and have
found new life and joy in Jesus Christ our Saviour. Will you accept
my terms?"

The atheist Lewis could only walk silently away! He knew as well as
anyone that only this Bible has the power to transform lives! Absolute
truth is universal; it is applicable everywhere, at any time, and in any
group of people. The Bible is applicable everywhere, at any moment,
and among any people simply because the Bible is absolute truth.

Writer George Bernard Shaw was a brilliant man, yet he rejected
the message of Scripture. Shortly before Shaw died in 1950, he wrote,

The science to which I pinned my faith is bankrupt. Its counsels,
which should have established the millennium, have led directly
to the suicide of Europe. I believed them once. In their name
I helped to destroy the faith of millions. And now they look at
me and witness the great tragedy of an atheist who has lost his
faith.

If the Bible is the Word of the One True God, then it should be
possible to find things written there that only God could have known.
Some of the external evidences of the Bible's authenticity include its
scientific, prophetical and historical statements. Just think, if you were
writing a book to fool people that you said was from God, you would be
silly to put in falsifiable data such as historical names and places. Certainly,
the last thing you would do is make clear statements about undiscovered
science and make prophecies hundreds of years in advance! With this in
mind, let us turn to see how the Bible matches up.

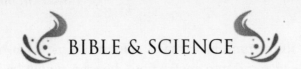

BIBLE & SCIENCE

A YOUNG MAN WHO WISHES TO REMAIN a sound atheist cannot be too careful of his reading.

C.S. Lewis, Christian apologist and author

Not only does the Bible contain many examples of fundamental science, but also it is as much as 3,500 years ahead of mankind's discovery of it. Throughout history, whenever the Bible has contradicted science the Bible is not the one that has had to change!

If you were to read a science textbook from 50 or 100 years ago, you would be amazed to discover the number of things that were stated as scientific fact, which are now known to be wrong! For example, 100 years ago it was emphatically stated by eminent scientists like Rutherford, that the atom could not be split. However, we now know, as do the survivors of Hiroshima and Nagasaki, that it can be split, and with terrifying results!

This reminds me of the story of the period that Einstein was active as a professor when one of his students came to him and said: "The questions of this year's exam are the same as last years!" "True," Einstein said, "but this year all the answers are different."

The Bible is not a science textbook but whatever the Bible says about science, history, geography, or anything else, it is true because God is the Author.

There are many examples of scientific truths in the Bible but I have chosen what I think are eleven of the simplest to understand. I have sought to distil the facts and scientific terms down for clarity.

1. "Thus the heavens and the earth were finished, and all the host of them"(Genesis 2:1).

It is interesting that Moses 3,450 years ago chose the Hebrew past definite tense for the verb "finished", indicating an action completed in the past, never again to occur. The Bible declared from the beginning that creation is complete (see Isa. 51:6, Psa. 102:26, and Heb. 1:11), God rested from his work (Gen. 2:2) and is still at rest (Heb. 4:4). This is a perfect correlation to the First Law of Thermodynamics (first formulated in the 1840's by Robert Mayer), which states that the total of all mass and energy in the universe remains constant. One form of energy or mass may be changed into another, but the total cannot be increased or decreased. In short, no new matter (energy) is coming into existence and its creation is complete.

2. "In the sweat of thy face shalt thou eat bread, till thou return unto the ground; for out of it wast thou taken: for dust thou art, and unto dust shalt thou return" (Gen. 3:19).

According to chemistry, the constituent elements of the human body are the same as those found in the earth. We should note carefully that 3,500 years ago when Moses wrote this, it was not known that the body had the same molecular composition as the ordinary dust on the ground.

3. "And when he that hath an issue is cleansed of his issue; then he shall number to himself seven days for his cleansing, and wash his clothes, and bathe his flesh in running water, and shall be clean" (Leviticus 15:13).

God gave His people specific instructions to regulate their behaviour when they encounter disease some 3,500 years before the germ concept of disease was discovered. Until recent years, doctors washed their hands in a bowl of water, leaving invisible germs on their hands resulting in the death of multitudes. We now know that doctors must wash their hands under running water as the Bible stated. The Bible also advises on the effect of emotions on physical health (Prov. 16:24; 17:22), quarantine control of contagious diseases (Lev. 13) and the importance of burial precautions, sanitation and sewage control to health (Num. 19: Deut. 23:12-13).[95]

4. "for the life of all flesh is the blood thereof" (Leviticus 17:14)

We know today that "the life of the flesh is in the blood" but it wasn't until after 1616, when Harvey discovered the role of blood circulation, that we learned that blood sustains life. Proverbs 14:30 complement's this revelation by describing the important role of the heart in this process when it states "A sound heart is the life of the flesh."

After Harvey's discovery the horrendous practice of bloodletting began to decline rapidly. Until then, perhaps millions of people had died due to physicians trying to "bleed" diseases out of them. One of the most famous of these was the first President of the USA, George Washington who died in 1799 from a fatal bloodletting procedure inflicted by his doctors.

5. "He stretcheth out the north over the empty place, and hangeth the earth upon nothing." (Job 26:7)

The Bible spoke of the earth's free float in space, which is a well-known fact today. The earth literally "hangeth upon nothing". At the time the book of Job was written, many of the heathen nations believed that the earth was supported by a giant man called Atlas. In fact, the Greeks believed it was by horses, elephants or snakes.

6. "He sealeth up the hand of every man; that all men may know his work." (Job 37:7)

As far back as 300 B.C. the Chinese used fingerprinting for official documents, land sales, contracts, loans and acknowledgments of debts. There is no certain evidence that the Chinese were aware of the uniqueness of a fingerprint. It is much more probable that they believed that physical contact with documents had some spiritual significance.

It wasn't until 150 years ago that it was definitely recorded that every person in the world has a unique fingerprint. This led Sir Edward Henry in 1901 to devise a workable classification system when appointed Assistant Commissioner of Police at Scotland Yard in London. The first British court conviction by fingerprints was obtained in 1902. The Bible tells us this amazing fact 3,500 years ago that God has put a seal on the hands of every man that can show crimes they have committed.

7. "It is he that sitteth upon the circle of the earth, and the inhabitants thereof are as grasshoppers; that stretcheth out the heavens as a curtain, and spreadeth them out as a tent to dwell in" (Isaiah 40:22)

The Hebrew word Isaiah used for "circle" means literally something with "roundness" or "spherically". Of course, the people of Isaiah's time (and for many generations to come) thought the earth was flat, not spherical. The book of Isaiah was written around 740 and 680 B.C. This is at least 300 years before Aristotle suggested, in his book On the Heavens, that the earth might be a sphere. It was another 2,000 years later (at a time when much of science maintained that the earth was flat) that the Scriptures inspired Christopher Columbus[96] to sail around the world as he records in his diary.

In 1916, Albert Einstein's mathematical Theory of General Relativity predicted an expanding universe from a single point beginning. The majority of observational evidence subsequently has validated Einstein's model that the universe is expanding and that it expanded from a single point. At this beginning point of the universe it should be noted that it did not emerge from existing material but "nothing." Before this point there was no space, time or matter – all of these came into existence at one moment in time just like the Bible described.

The Hebrew in this passage indicates that God's work in stretching out the heavens is both "finished" and "ongoing". Here we find two different verbs used "stretcheth" and "spreadeth" in two different forms to indicate two different works. This one verse literally states that God is both continuing to stretch out the heavens and has stretched them out. This is exactly what we see today with a simultaneously finished and ongoing aspect of cosmic expansion.

8. "the host of heaven cannot be numbered" (Jeremiah 33:22, Genesis 22:17)

For centuries, scholars thought that the stars were very limited in number and could be counted without a great deal of trouble. Hipparchus, in 150 B.C., said that there were less than 3,000 stars. Ptolemy, the famed astronomer of Egypt in 150 A.D., said he had counted precisely 1,056 stars. Yet Jeremiah 33:22, which was written 2,600 years ago, told us that: "the host of heaven cannot be numbered." It was not until Galileo invented the telescope (1608 A.D.) that science realized the stars were innumerable. It is now believed that the universe contains at least 70 sextillion or 70 thousand million million million observable stars!

9. "His going forth is from the end of the heaven, and his circuit unto the ends of it: and there is nothing hid from the heat there of." (Psalm 19:4;6)

For many years, Bible critics mocked the Bible that this verse taught the old myth that the sun revolves around the earth! However, it was recently discovered that the sun is in fact, moving through space. It is not stationary, as was once thought. In fact, it is estimated to be moving in a gigantic orbit in the Milky Way galaxy through space at about 486,000 miles per hour,[97] in an orbit so large it would take an estimated 226 million years just to complete one orbit! The Milky Way galaxy itself is moving among the other galaxies. So the circuit of the sun is, indeed, from one end of the heavens to the other.

10. "And, Thou, Lord, in the beginning hast laid the foundation of the earth; and the heavens are the works of thine hands: They shall perish; but Thou remainest; and they all shall wax old as doth a garment" (Hebrews 1:10,11)

Although the Bible recorded the aging and wearing out of the earth 2,000 years ago, it was not until the 1800's that the validation of the Second Law of Thermodynamics (the Law of Entropy) confirmed the accuracy of this statement. Although there is a constant amount of energy in the universe, in all kinds of energy transferences there is a loss of useful energy. For example, in creating heat, the sun is diminishing at the rate of 4,600,000[98] tons per second! And it is not just the sun; the Law of Entropy says all things are growing older, wearing out, running down and decaying.

The concept of entropy has been developed to describe this phenomenon, entropy being a measure of the unavailability of the energy of the system or process. Or, in more general terms, the second law states that there is always a tendency for any system to become less organized. Its disorder or randomness tends to increase. If isolated from external sources of order or energy or "information," any system will eventually run down and "cease." No exception to the second law of thermodynamics has ever been found!

11. "Through faith we understand that the worlds were framed by the word of God, so that things which are seen were not made of things which do appear." (Hebrews 11:3)

Up until a century ago, science had not discovered for certain that all matter consists of very small, indivisible atomic particles that were invisible to the naked eye. Dalton proposed the atomic theory in 1808 but it wasn't until 110 years ago when German physicist, W.C. Roentgen discovered the X-ray and in the 1930's when the electron microscope came into existence that this was certified. The Bible says matter that is "seen" was "not made of things which do appear." In simple terms, the universe that we can measure and detect was made out of that which we cannot measure or detect.

Conclusion

The particles that make up the nucleus of the atom are so charged that they should repel each other to the degree that every atom in the universe ought to result in an atomic explosion! However, scientists have discovered what they call are "strong" and "weak forces" that they cannot explain, which holds atoms together and keeps them from exploding. The Bible says this mysterious "force" is Christ that is keeping the universe from flying apart (Colossians 1:17).

Just think for a moment, the reason you are able to exist and read this book right now is because Christ is maintaining this atomic stability. If we were to draw to scale the nucleus of the atom as a few centimetres the surrounding electron field around it would be at least 4 miles wide with nothing in between. As Professor of Theoretical Physics at Adelaide University, Paul Davies marvelled:

The really amazing thing is not that life on Earth is balanced on a knife-edge, but that the entire universe is balanced on a knife-edge, and would be total chaos if any of the natural "constants" were off even slightly.....even if you dismiss man as a chance happening, the fact remains that the universe seems unreasonably suited to the existence of life - almost contrived - you might say a "put-up job."

Some sceptics claim that some of the many ancient non-Christian writers made claims similar to those set out above. While this may be true in some instances, only the Bible can claim to be perfectly accurate in so many and considering its diverse authorship that spans a period of 1,500 years, this is truly amazing! No other major world religion can make this claim!

THE BIBLE, PROPHECY, & HISTORY

I HAVE LIVED, SIR, A LONG TIME, and the longer I live, the more convincing proofs I see of this truth -- that God Governs the affairs of men. And if a sparrow cannot fall to the ground without His notice, is it probable that an empire can rise without His aid?
Benjamin Franklin

The Bible was written over a period of 1,500 years with more than 40 authors. Its authorship was diverse, yet its unity is amazing. More than 30% of the Bible is prophecy – no other religious book can make this claim! There are no prophecies in the Qur'an, Hindu Vedas or Bhagavad-Gita, Book of Mormon, writings of Buddha or Confucius.[99]

John Blanchard in his classic book Does God believe in Atheists[100] gives three examples of fulfilled prophecy from the hundreds of examples (many that were made centuries in advance):

Around 920 BC, an unnamed prophet told Jeroboam, who was King of Israel, that his throne would one day be occupied by a King called Josiah, who would sweep away the widespread idolatry which Jeroboam was promoting. This must have seemed nonsensical to the all-powerful Jeroboam at the time, but 300 years later Josiah was enthroned on the death of his father and began to carry out the programme the prophet had predicted.[101]

Isaiah, who prophesied for forty years from about 740 BC, predicted a whole series of future events, including the downfall of Jerusalem and the wholesale deportation of the Jews to Babylon. Even more remarkably, he prophesied that their captivity would be ended by someone called Cyrus, who would repatriate the Jews for the specific purpose of rebuilding the temple at Jerusalem. Exactly as forecast, the Babylonians sacked Jerusalem and swept the Jews into captivity. In 539-538 BC, nearly 200 years after

Isaiah's prophecy, the pagan King of Persia conquered Babylon and as one of his first acts, released all foreigners the Babylonians had captured, with specific instructions to the Jews that they return to Jerusalem and rebuild their temple. The pagan King's name? Cyrus![102]

Around 600 BC, Habakkuk prophesied that the Chaldeans would be the future masters of the world. This must have seemed absurd at the time, as the Chaldeans formed an insignificant group of people in Babylon, which had by then become the major world power. Only Egypt seemed likely to pose any future threat to Assyria, and even that was a long shot, yet within a few years the Chaldeans had fulfilled Habakkuk's prophecy to the letter.[103]

Other examples include:

1. Amos 1:3-5
   Damascus will be conquered
   Tiglath-Pileser (732 BC)
2. Amos 1:6-8
   Gaza, Ashdod, and Askelon will be destroyed
   Several different armies
3. Amos 1:9-10
   Tyre will be destroyed by fire
   Sargon II (722 BC)
4. Amos 2:1-3
   Moab will be burned and the judge removed
   Nebuchadnezzar (582 BC)
5. Amos 2:4-5
   Jerusalem will be destroyed
   Nebuchadnezzar (586 BC)
6. Amos 3:12-15; Micah 1:6
   Samaria will be destroyed
   Sargon II (722 BC)
7. Micah 5:2
   The Messiah will be born in Bethlehem
   Luke 2
8. Zechariah 9:9
   A king shall come to Jerusalem

Matthew 21:4-5
9. Malachi 4:5
   Elijah will come again
   Matthew 11:14; Mark 9:11-12
10. Matthew 24:1-3
    Temple will be destroyed
    Romans in AD 70
11. Luke 19:41-44
    Jerusalem will be destroyed
    Romans in AD 70

(Abridged from Protestant Christian Evidences by Bernard Ramm, Moody Press, 1953, p. 81-124.)

One commentator has said that the greatest evidence for the Bible was the Jews. For, no group of people has suffered more ridicule, persecution and genocide than this group. Yet where ever you find them in this world they survive and prosper just as the Bible said. "And in thy seed shall all the nations of the earth be blessed;"Genesis 22:18. "Therefore ye are my witnesses, saith the LORD, that I am God" Isaiah 43:12. "For I am with thee, saith the LORD, to save thee: though I make a full end of all nations whither I have scattered thee, yet will I not make a full end of thee:" Jeremiah 30:11.

From a pool of 14 million Jews (around 0.2 % of the World's population) has emanated 164 Nobel Prizes out of the total 700 or so that have been awarded. It cannot be bias as these prizes are awarded by Swedish Gentile judges and they span literature, economics, peace and science. Jews prosper in industry such as Chelsea football club owner Roman Abramovich, Marks & Spencer, Calvin Klein, Warburgs, and Rothschilds and so on. For instance, it is estimated that despite making up less than 1% of the population of the USA about one-third of the faculty at Harvard Medical School is Jewish. Other examples are that every 9th senator in the Senate of 108th Congress was Jewish in January 2003 and there are twenty-six Jewish Congressmen currently in the House of Representatives.

The Bible predicted in 800 BC that the Jews would return to Israel which they did in 1948 and re-capture the city of Jerusalem which they did on 7th June 1967:

And I will bring again the captivity of my people of Israel, and they shall build the waste cities, and inhabit them; and they shall

plant vineyards, and drink the wine thereof; they shall also make gardens, and eat the fruit of them. And I will plant them upon their land, and they shall no more be pulled up out of their land which I have given them, saith the LORD thy God.
Amos 9:15

Thus saith the LORD of hosts; Behold, I will save my people from the east country, and from the west country; And I will bring them, and they shall dwell in the midst of Jerusalem: and they shall be my people, and I will be their God, in truth and in righteousness.
Zechariah 8:7-8

The Bible has been attacked more than any other book, yet it remains the most historically accurate book of ancient history on the planet. Thanks to archeological discoveries over the past two centuries, sceptics have been embarrassed repeatedly, yet they never seem to give up. For instance, in the nineteenth century, sceptics frequently argued Moses couldn't have written the first five books of the Bible because writing hadn't been invented yet (c. 1400 B.C.) However, excavations in 1964 of the ancient city of Ebla (found in modern Syria) unearthed some 17,000 written clay tablets. Ebla was destroyed in 2250 B.C.!

Christianity is unique in that it is built on historical events recorded in the Bible and can therefore be proved to be historically accurate by investigation. Geography, place names, people, and historical events in the Bible have been found to be correct and accurate. Many of these have been discovered by archaeologists in the last two centuries. The renowned archaeologist William F. Albright stated:

There can be no doubt that archaeology has confirmed the substantial historicity of the Old Testament tradition.[104]

Some examples of these discoveries include:

1. Lot's family and city of Zoar (Genesis 19:18-22)
   Name of Lots family and city of Zoar found on tablet unearthed in Ebla in 1964 excavation
2. Sargon, king of Assyria (Isaiah 20:1)
   His palace was discovered in 1843 by Paul Botta.
3. King Mesha (2 Kings 3:4)

He is mentioned in an inscription called the Moabite or Mesha Stone that was discovered in 1869 by F A Klein.

4. Sennacharib, king of Assyria (2 Kings 18, 19; 2 Chronicles 32)
   A large hexagonal prism was discovered which describes his ex ploits including the siege of Jerusalem and King Hezekiah.

5. Shalmaneser, king of Assyria (2 Kings 17:3-6)
   He left an obelisk describing his life which includes a carving of Jehu, king of Israel paying tribute.

6. Cyrus, king of Persia (2 Chronicles 36:22-23)
   Made a decree, which allowed captive people to return to their homes. A cylinder with an inscription of the decree is in the British Museum

7. Belshazzar, King of Babylon (Daniel 5:16,29)
   In 1882 the discovery of the Chronicle of Nabonidus confirmed this.

THE PHENOMENON OF JESUS CHRIST

I AM AN HISTORIAN, I AM NOT A BELIEVER, but I must confess as a historian that this penniless preacher from Nazareth is irrevocably the very center of history. Jesus Christ is easily the most dominant figure in all history.
H.G. Wells, English author

Just as the scientific, prophetical and historical statements of the preceding chapters show the Bible is the Word of the One True God, so we can be confident that what it says about the return of Jesus Christ and about us is also true. The Bible clearly teaches that Jesus is coming back soon and He will destroy this world and judge every person on this earth for his or her sins.

At the heart of every religion there is a leading personality. Mohammed says the Qu'ran is the "truth as God showed me," Buddha says his Noble Truths "enlighten you" and Confucius says his teachings "instruct you." In fact, Buddha's disciples before he died asked him how they should remember him. "Never mind about me," he replied, "remember my teachings." It is one of the unique features of Jesus Christ, however, that He always directed people to Himself. He was "the Word" and He was "the Way."

Jesus Christ was the most remarkable man who ever lived. Unlike all the other founders of world religions, He never sinned. Mohammed expressly asked for forgiveness of his sins:

> Oh God, I acknowledge and confess before You, all my sins, please forgive them, as no one can forgive sins except You. Forgive my mistakes, those done intentionally, or out of my ignorance, with or without seriousness.[105]

Confucius at the close of his life said:

> In letters I am perhaps equal to other men; but the character of the perfect man, carrying out in his conduct what he professes, is what I have not yet attained to.[106]

Jesus is Life! He is Light! He is the Living Water! He is the Bread of Life!

An atheist, hearing the testimony of converted drunkard, blurted out in scorn, "It is nothing, I tell you. It's just foolishness, and a figment of the imagination; that is all. It is nothing but an escape from reality-a dream!" Looking down, the atheist saw the bewildered eyes of a small child.

"Please, sir," she said with a sob, "if he is dreaming, don't wake him up. He's been so good to us since he met Jesus. You see, he is my daddy." Small wonder that the atheist turned away with no answer.

A lady came to me once and said, "I am searching for the truth." I told her that she had come to the right person "because I have found the Truth – His name is Jesus."

No other religious leader ever revealed God to mankind in all His fullness like Jesus did. You never hear Moslems singing about Mohammed, "I am thine O Mohammed." No Buddhist ever sings, "Buddha, lover of my soul." No Confucian ever sings, "All that thrills my soul is Confucius." No other religious leader rose from the dead – their tombs are still marked and with us, except the Prophet from Nazareth!

And the day Jesus Christ rose from the grave on the first Easter morning almost two thousand years ago was the one moment in all history that changed the world. No other religious leader or any indeed any other leader ever claimed such a triumph over the grave.

Jesus Christ never left a record of his birth, yet we link our calendars to it; never wrote a book, yet is the subject of more books than any other person; limited his preaching to a small country for just over three years, yet his followers are in every corner of this world; never formed an army, yet millions have laid down their lives in his service. How can atheism explain this unprecedented phenomenon?

French Emperor, Napoleon Bonaparte summed up the uniqueness of Jesus Christ when he said:

> I know men, and I tell you Jesus Christ was not a man. Superficial minds see a resemblance between Christ and the founders of empires and the gods of other religions. That resemblance does not exist. There is between Christianity and other religions the distance of infinity. Alexander, Caesar, Charlemagne, and myself founded empires; but what foundation did we rest the creations of our genius? Upon force. Jesus Christ founded an empire upon love; and at this hour millions of men would die for Him.

Famed Hindu leader, Mahatma Ghandi also marvelled:

> A man who was completely innocent, offered himself as a sacrifice for the good of others, including his enemies, and became the ransom of the world. It was a perfect act.

Even the world-renowned physicist, Albert Einstein could not hide his admiration for Jesus Christ:

> As a child I received instruction both in the Bible and in the Talmud. I am a Jew, but I am enthralled by the luminous figure of the Nazarene . . . . No one can read the Gospels without feeling the actual presence of Jesus. His personality pulsates in every word. No myth is filled with such life.

The ultimate tribute to the power of the gospel and the fear that Jesus Christ is real is even seen in the homes of the most ardent atheistic communists. Gary Thomas of Christianity Today describes:

> As Vice President, George Bush represented the U.S. at the funeral of former Soviet leader Leonid Brezhnev. Bush was deeply moved by a silent protest carried out by Brezhnev's widow. She stood motionless by the coffin until seconds before it was closed. Then, just as the soldiers touched the lid, Brezhnev's wife performed an act of great courage and hope, a gesture that must surely rank as one of the most profound acts of civil disobedience ever committed: She reached down and made the sign of the cross on her husband's chest. There in the citadel of secular, atheistic power, the wife of the man who had run it all hoped that her husband was wrong. She hoped that there was another life, and

that that life was best represented by Jesus who died on the cross, and that the same Jesus might yet have mercy on her husband.[107]

Mao Zedong's wife Jiang Qing told foreign visitors to China in the 1970's: "Christianity in China has been confined to the history section of the museum. It is dead and buried."

In the 1970's another visiting Christian delegation from the United States was told, "There is not a single Christian left in China." Today China has the fastest growing church in the world with tens of millions of Christians. However, the Bible promises in Numbers 23:19 that "God is not a man, that he should lie; .....hath he said, and shall he not do it."

Since the 1970s the growth of the church in China has been nothing short of amazing. Bearing in mind that as recently as 1978 all churches were closed down, Christianity was effectively outlawed and an atheistic education was mandated for all, China has seen maybe the most glorious revival in world history. Even in the Government controlled Three Self Patriotic Movement (TSPM) churches, many of which have little or no gospel to offer the hungry seeking souls, are crowded week by week. For instance, in a 1999 report, the Chinese Government statistics for the TSPM numbered Protestant Christians who are baptized adherents as 13 million: 13,000 Churches; 27,000 Meeting points;13 million Protestant Christians (not including those not yet registered.); 500,000-600,000 new baptisms per year; 1,000 plus Seminary or Bible college students; 1,300 Pastors (300 women).

The TSPM Report by their Amity News Service[108] also stated the following:

> In 1949, when the People's Republic of China was established, there were less than one million Protestants in the entire country. Today, the rapid increase in believers has led pundits to use the term "Christianity fever". The provinces of Zhejiang and Jiangsu provide cases in point.
>
> The population of Zhejiang is 2.8% Christian, probably the highest percentage on the mainland. Its Christian population doubled in the last ten years, from 600,000 in 1988 to 1.3 million today. Nine percent of the population of the city of Wenzhou and 12% of Dongtou County is Christian. If all of China had the same percentage of Christians as Zhejiang, there would be

33 million Protestant Christians in China.

In Jiangsu, the number of Protestant Christians increased sevenfold In the decade between 1985 and 1995, from 125,000 in 1985 to 400,000 in 1989, to 900,000 in 1995. Today, there are one million believers in the province.

It is reasonable to assume that these claims and statistics are accurate as they are from a government source that would have no interest in inflating them. It should also be noted that these figures do not include those who attend the TSPM churches but are not adherents, children under the age of 18 or the millions of believers who meet in unregistered house churches.

Another telling statistic is that the number of legal Bibles that have been printed by the TSPM since 1987 has now passed the 40 million mark.[109] The Communist Government limits the numbers available each year by Amity Press but it is suggestive that already 40 million have been printed and millions more have been smuggled in or printed illegally. In the city I worked in many house churches use Bibles printed illegally in China.

Beatles singer John Lennon once boasted on March 4, 1966: "Christianity will go. It will vanish and shrink. I needn't argue with that; I'm right and I will be proved right. We're more popular than Jesus now."

Lennon is dead, by and large forgotten, but the person and work of Jesus Christ goes marching on! He is going forward "conquering, and to conquer." There is no one to compare to Jesus Christ. He stands head and shoulders above all history and He bridges all eternity.

IF I WERE ASKED TODAY THE MAIN CAUSE OF THE RUINOUS REVOLUTION that has swallowed up some sixty million of our people, I could not put it more accurately than to repeat: "Men have forgotten God; that's why all this has happened."

Alexander Solzhenitsyn, dissident Soviet authoer

Part 4

WHAT DOES GOD SAY ABOUT YOU?

THE SIX FACTS OF LIFE

I WANT ATHEISM TO BE TRUE and am made uneasy by the fact that some of the most intelligent and well-informed people I know are religious believers. It isn't just that I don't believe in God and, naturally, I hope that I'm right in my belief. It's that I hope there is no God! I don't want there to be a God; I don't want the universe to be like that.

Thomas Nagel, Professor of Philosophy and Law at New York University

FACT 1 – God makes the rules – your opinions don't count

It does not matter what your opinion is about God or the Bible at this point – they are facts. You may not believe that the sun will rise or that the tide will come in, but tomorrow the sun will rise and the tide will come in.

If you want to become a British Citizen, you have to follow the rules laid down in law by the U.K. Government. It is not enough for you to satisfy 50% of the requirements and then think that you can ignore the rest or try a different way to satisfy them. You will fail completely in your objective – and rightly so!

When it come to getting to heaven, the same principle is true. We don't make the rules or the terms and conditions. Only God does and He is very clear about them. Don't argue with me, I didn't write them – He did! There is no appeals process.

FACT 2 – We are all sinners

You are not here by accident. God wants you to have a personal relationship with Him. There is just one thing that separates you from God. That one thing is your sin. People tend to divide themselves into groups of good and bad. But God says that every person that has ever lived is a sinner, and any sin separates us from God. That includes you and me. "For all have sinned and come short of the glory of God." Romans 3:23

We are all born with a sinful nature. This is obvious as you don't have to teach a child how to lie, steal, be disobedient to their parent's etc.

FACT 3 – The punishment for our sin is death

All citizens accept people should be punished for breaking their national laws. God says that the punishment for our sins (or breaking His law) is death: "For the wages of sin is death; but the gift of God is eternal life through Jesus Christ our Lord." Romans 6:23

Movie Director and atheist, Woody Allen declared, "I don't want to be immortal through my work. I want to be immortal through not dying." – sorry Woody, but the latest statistics (and these are taken from a 6,000 year sample) show that out of 100 people – 100 die!

Statistics also show: rich and poor die, powerful and weak die, all races die, all nationalities die, doctors and nurses die and even atheistic scientists die (whether they believe it or not!) – no one escapes the curse of death!

FACT 4 – You cannot take away the sin problem by yourself

If you look all around, you will see that many are working hard to take their sins away. Some people go to temples, others try praying, fasting, attending church, confessing to a priest, burning incense and giving to the poor. However, God makes the rules of salvation (not any man or church) and the Bible says it is only God's grace that allows you to come to Him - not your efforts to "clean up your life" or work your way to Heaven. You can't earn it. It's a free gift. "For by grace are ye saved through faith; and that not of yourselves: it is the gift of God: Not of works, lest any man should boast." Ephesians 2:8;9 Note: salvation is "not of yourselves" and "not of works."

FACT 5 – God has made a way for you to have your sins taken away

God knows you are a sinner and cannot take away your sins. This is why because of His great love He sent Jesus to die for our sins. "For God so loved the world, that he gave his only begotten Son, that whosoever believeth in him should not perish, but have everlasting life." John 3:16

Jesus paid the price for our sins by giving His life on Calvary's cross.

God brought Jesus back from the dead and made the way for you to have a personal relationship with Him only through Jesus.

FACT 6 – You must accept the free gift by faith only to have eternal life

I cannot force you to become a Christian – it is your choice. If I offer you $1000 gift you can either accept or reject it. To become a Christian all that's left for you to do is to accept the gift that Jesus is holding out for you right now. "That if thou shalt confess with thy mouth the Lord Jesus, and shalt believe in thine heart that God hath raised him from the dead, thou shalt be saved." Romans 10:9

Are you ready to accept the gift of eternal life that Jesus is offering you right now? If it is your sincere desire to ask Jesus to come into your heart as your personal Lord and Saviour, then talk to God from your heart:

Here's a Suggested Prayer:

Lord Jesus, I know that I am a sinner and I do not deserve eternal life. I know that I cannot do anything to take away my sins. But, I believe You died and rose from the grave to purchase a place in Heaven for me. I want to turn away and repent from my sins. I ask you right now Jesus, to come into my life, be King of my life, forgive my sins and save me. I am now placing my trust in You alone for my salvation and I accept your free gift of eternal life.

If you have done this then God has promised (not me or the church) that you "shall not perish but have everlasting life" (John 3:16).

On the other hand, maybe you are like atheist, Robert G. Ingersoll at this point and still reject the best offer you will ever get. He said in his foolish pride:

I want no heaven for which I must give my reason; no happiness in exchange for my liberty, and no immortality that demands the surrender of my individuality. Better rot in the windowless tomb, to which there is no door but the red mouth of the pallid worm, than to wear the jeweled collar of a god.

Remember, just as every choice we make in life there is a consequence. The consequence of rejecting the free offer of the gospel is that you go to hell when you die - forever and ever. Voltaire the leading European atheist of his day cried on his deathbed: "I am abandoned by God and man; I shall go to hell! I will give you half of what I am worth, if you will give me six month's life."

We may never meet on earth but we definitely will meet at the end of this world because God says that one day very soon we will all stand before God to be judged for our sins and the consequences of rejecting Jesus Christ is spelt out clearly:

> And I saw the dead, small and great, stand before God; and the books were opened: and another book was opened, which is the book of life: and the dead were judged out of those things which were written in the books, according to their works. And the sea gave up the dead which were in it; and death and hell delivered up the dead which were in them: and they were judged every man according to their works. ....And whosoever was not found written in the book of life was cast into the lake of fire.
>
> Revelation 20: 12;13;15

Christianity is fair. The way to heaven is the same for everyone and does not require you to do a range of rituals and examinations. Whether you are educated or uneducated, literate or illiterate, rich or poor, famous or unknown you can find the way. It is a wonderfully simple way and open to everyone who is willing to believe!

Now, my words must end. Logic has done all it can to satisfy your intellect – now it is a question of your will. The evidence for God's existence is not an obstacle to your salvation – YOU are!

WHAT IS YOUR DECISION?

THERE ARE ONLY TWO KINDS OF PEOPLE IN THE END: those who say to God, "Thy will be done," and those to whom God says, in the end, "Thy will be done."
C.S. Lewis

Part 5

APPENDICES

APPENDIX 1
TESTIMONIES OF FAITH

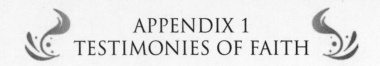

These testimonies are from some of those students of mine that have been touched by the power of this Jesus of Nazareth. Almost 2,000 years have passed since He walked this earth, yet the man of Galilee is still opening the eyes of the blind and bringing life. This is the greatest miracle of all.

I was brought up in Guangzhou province in China and before I came to Singapore I had never heard the gospel. I had believed till this time that there was no God. I first heard the gospel when my English lecturer, Paul explained about God and the proofs for his existence in February 2005 in class. A few weeks later at a gospel meeting at Jesus Saves Mission in Singapore, I received Jesus as my Saviour. It has changed my life and given me a reason for living. My friend has also got saved at the end of June.

Grace, Chinese student

My name is Thanh and I was born and educated in Vietnam. Although my family followed the Buddhist faith, I was in reality an atheist until I came to Singapore in 2004. I first heard about Jesus from my teacher, Paul and his wife. After attending a church in Singapore with them in April 2005, I accepted Jesus Christ as my Saviour at their house. It is my hope and prayer that I can reach my family and friends with the gospel. Some of my friends have already come to church with me.

Faith Thanh, Vietnamese student

My name is Thao and when I came to Singapore I had never heard about Jesus. In fact, I was an atheist. My teacher Paul was the first one to tell me about Jesus. It was after a gospel meeting when my teacher spoke at in a church on 19th March 2005 that I accepted Jesus into my heart. It was the first time I had been in a Christian Church. Jesus has given me confidence and real meaning to my life. I have since shared the gospel with my cousin and she also has become a Christian and attends church with me.

Mercy Thao, Vietnamese student

APPENDIX 2
THE PROFESSOR AND THE CHRISTIAN

"Let me explain the problem science has with Jesus Christ." The atheist professor of philosophy pauses before his class and then asks one of his new students to stand. "You're a Christian, aren't you, son?"

"Yes, sir."

"So you believe in God?"

"Absolutely."

"Is God good?"

"Sure! God's good."

"Is God all-powerful? Can God do anything?"

"Yes."

"Are you good or evil?"

"The Bible says I'm evil."

The professor grins knowingly. "Ahh! THE BIBLE!" He considers for a moment. "Here's one for you. Let's say there's a sick person over here and you can cure him. You can do it. Would you help them? Would you try?"

"Yes sir, I would."

"So you're good...!"

"I wouldn't say that."

"Why not say that? You would help a sick and maimed person if you could.... in fact most of us would if we could...God doesn't."

[No answer.]

"He doesn't, does he? My brother was a Christian who died of cancer even though he prayed to Jesus to heal him. How is this Jesus good? Hmmm? Can you answer that one?"

[No answer]

The elderly man is sympathetic. "No, you can't, can you?" He takes a sip of water from a glass on his desk to give the student time to relax. In philosophy, you have to go easy with the new ones. "Let's start again, young fella."

"Is God good?"

"Er... Yes."

"Is Satan good?"

"No."

"Where does Satan come from?"

The student falters. "From... God..."

"That's right. God made Satan, didn't he?" The elderly man runs his bony fingers through his thinning hair and turns to the smirking, student audience. "I think we're going to have a lot of fun this semester, ladies and gentlemen." He turns back to the Christian. "Tell me, son. Is there evil in this world?"

"Yes, sir."

"Evil's everywhere, isn't it? Did God make everything?"

"Yes."

"Who created evil?"

[No answer]

"Is there sickness in this world? Immorality? Hatred? Ugliness? All the terrible things - do they exist in this world?"

The student squirms on his feet. "Yes."

"Who created them?"

[No answer]

The professor suddenly shouts at his student. "WHO CREATED THEM? TELL ME, PLEASE! "The professor closes in for the kill and climbs into the Christian's face. In a still small voice: "God created all evil, didn't He, son?"

[No answer]

The student tries to hold the steady, experienced gaze and fails. Suddenly the lecturer breaks away to pace the front of the classroom like an aging panther. The class is mesmerized.

"Tell me," he continues, "how is it that this God is good if He created all evil throughout all time?" The professor swishes his arms around to encompass the wickedness of the world. "All the hatred, the brutality, all the pain, all the torture, all the death and ugliness and all the suffering created by this good God is all over the world, isn't it, young man?"

[No answer]

"Don't you see it all over the place? Huh?"

Pause.

"Don't you?" The professor leans into the student's face again and whispers, "Is God good?"

[No answer]

"Do you believe in Jesus Christ, son?"

The student's voice betrays him and cracks. "Yes, professor. I do."

The old man shakes his head sadly. "Science says you have five senses you use to identify and observe the world around you. Have you seen your Jesus?"

"No, sir. I've never seen Him."

"Then tell us if you've ever heard your Jesus?"

"No, sir. I have not."

"Have you ever felt your Jesus, tasted your Jesus or smelt your Jesus... in fact, do you have any sensory perception of your God whatsoever?"

[No answer]

"Answer me, please."

"No, sir, I'm afraid I haven't."

"You're AFRAID... you haven't?"

"No, sir."

"Yet you still believe in him?"

"...yes..."

"That takes FAITH!" The professor smiles sagely at the underling. "According to the rules of empirical, testable, demonstrable protocol, science says your God doesn't exist. What do you say to that, son? Where is your God now?"

[The student doesn't answer]

"Sit down, please." The Christian sits...Defeated.

Another Christian raises his hand. "Professor, may I address the class?"

The professor turns and smiles. "Ah, another Christian in the vanguard! Come, come, young man. Speak some proper wisdom to the gathering."

The Christian looks around the room. "Some interesting points you are making, sir. Now I've got a question for you. Is there such thing as heat?"

"Yes," the professor replies. "There's heat."

"Is there such a thing as cold?" "Yes, son, there's cold too."

"No, sir, there isn't."

The professor's grin freezes. The room suddenly goes very still. The second Christian continues. "You can have lots of heat, even more heat, super-heat, mega-heat, white heat, a little heat or no heat but we don't have anything called 'cold'. We can hit 458 degrees below zero, which is no heat, but we can't go any further after that. There is no such thing as cold, otherwise we would be able to go colder than minus 458. You see, sir, cold is only a word we use to describe the absence of heat. We cannot measure cold. Heat we can measure in thermal units because heat is energy. Cold is not the opposite of heat, sir, just the absence of it."

Silence. A pin drops somewhere in the classroom.

"Is there such a thing as darkness, professor?"

"That's a dumb question, son. What is night if it isn't darkness? What are you getting at...?"

"So you say there is such a thing as darkness?"

"Yes..."

"You're wrong again, sir. Darkness is not something, it is the absence of something. You can have low light, normal light, bright light, flashing light but if you have no light constantly you have nothing and it's called darkness, isn't it? That's the meaning we use to define the word. In reality, Darkness isn't. If it were, you would be able to make darkness darker and give me a jar of it. Can you...give me a jar of darker darkness, professor?"

Despite himself, the professor smiles at the young effrontery before him. This will indeed be a good semester. "Would you mind telling us what your point is, young man?"

"Yes, professor. My point is, your philosophical premise is flawed to start with and so your conclusion must be in error...."

The professor goes toxic. "Flawed...? How dare you...!"

"Sir, may I explain what I mean?"

The class is all ears. "Explain... oh, explain..." The professor makes an admirable effort to regain control. Suddenly he is affability itself. He waves his hand to silence the class, for the student to continue.

"You are working on the premise of duality," the Christian explains. "That for example there is life and then there's death; a good God and a bad God. You are viewing the concept of God as something finite, something we can measure. Sir, science cannot even explain a thought. It uses electricity and magnetism but has never seen, much less fully understood them. To view death as the opposite of life is to be ignorant of the fact that death cannot exist as a substantive thing. Death is not the opposite of life, merely the absence of it." The young man holds up a newspaper he takes from the desk of a neighbor who has been reading it. "Here is one of the most disgusting tabloids this country hosts, professor. Is there such a thing as immorality?"

"Of course there is, now look..."

"Wrong again, sir. You see, immorality is merely the absence of morality. Is there such thing as injustice? No. Injustice is the absence of justice. Is there such a thing as evil?" The Christian pauses. "Isn't evil the absence of good?" The professor's face has turned an alarming colour. He is so angry he is temporarily speechless. The Christian continues. "If there is evil in the world, professor, and we all agree there is, then God, if He exists, must be accomplishing a work through the agency of evil. What is that work, God is accomplishing? The Bible tells us it is to see if each one of us will, of our own free will, choose good over evil."

The professor bridles. "As a philosophical scientist, I don't view this matter as having anything to do with any choice; as a realist, I absolutely do not recognize the concept of God or any other theological factor as being part of the world equation because God is not observable."

"I would have thought that the absence of God's moral code in this world is probably one of the most observable phenomena going," the Christian replies. "Newspapers make billions of dollars reporting it every week! Tell me, professor. Do you teach your students that they evolved from a monkey?"

"If you are referring to the natural evolutionary process, young man, yes, of course I do."

"Have you ever observed evolution with your own eyes, sir?" The professor makes a sucking sound with his teeth and gives his student a silent, stony stare. "Professor. Since no one has ever observed the process of evolution at work and cannot even prove that this process is an on-going endeavour, are you not teaching your opinion, sir? Are you now not a scientist, but a priest?"

"I'll overlook your impudence in the light of our philosophical discussion. Now, have you quite finished?" the professor hisses.

"So you don't accept God's moral code to do what is righteous?"

"I believe in what is - that's science!"

"Ahh! SCIENCE!" the student's face splits into a grin. "Sir, you rightly state that science is the study of observed phenomena. Science too is a premise which is flawed..."

"SCIENCE IS FLAWED?..." the professor splutters.

The class is in uproar.

The Christian remains standing until the commotion has subsided. "To continue the point you were making earlier to the other student, may I give you an example of what I mean?" The professor wisely keeps silent. The Christian looks around the room. "Is there anyone in the class who has ever seen the professor's brain?"

The class breaks out in laughter. The Christian points towards his elderly, crumbling tutor. "Is there anyone here who has ever heard the professor's brain... felt the professor's brain, touched or smelt the professor's brain?"

No one appears to have done so. The Christian shakes his head sadly. "It appears no one here has had any sensory perception of the professor's brain whatsoever. Well, according to the rules of empirical, stable, demonstrable protocol, science, I DECLARE that the professor has no brain."

The class is in chaos.

The Christian sits... Because that is what a chair is for..

APPENDIX 3
THE PREACHER AND THE ATHEIST

The preacher was on the street corner telling the passing crowds about Jesus Christ. A crowd had gathered and was listening intently. Then a hoarse voice spoke up from the back.

"Preacher, you've got it all wrong. Atheism is the answer to humanity's problems. People get into trouble and go crazy when they hear about Christianity. Religion is bad for minds and ruins lives. Come on now,— prove to me that Christianity is real, and I'll be quiet." Everyone was interested to see what would happen next.

The preacher held up his hand for quiet, and then said this:

> Never did I hear anyone state, 'I was undone and an outcast, but I read Thomas Paine's Age of Reason and now I have been saved from the power of sin.' Never did I hear of one who declared, 'I was in darkness and despair and knew not where to turn, until I read Ingersoll's Lectures, and then found peace of heart and solutions to my problems.'

> 'Never did I hear an atheist telling that his atheism had been

the means by which he had been set free from the bondage of liquor. Never did I learn of anyone who conquered hard drugs by renouncing faith in God.' But I have heard many testify that, when as hopeless and helpless sinners, they had turned in their great need to the Son of God and cast themselves upon Him for forgiveness and enabling power to overcome sin—they were given peace of heart and victory over enslaving sin!

Then, turning to the atheist, he said:

Who starts the orphanages, the city missions, and the work among the poor? It is the Christians. Who owns and operates the taverns, and manufactures the liquor sold in them? It is the atheists. Who risk their lives to help poor people in mission fields all over the world? It is the Christians. Who runs the abortion mills and the houses of prostitution? It is the atheists. Who are the most solid, kindly, industrious people in the nation? It is the Christians. Who operates the gambling halls and the crime syndicates? It is the atheists. Who are the swindlers, bank robbers, and embezzlers? It is the atheists. Who helps men put away their sins, live to bless others, and prepares men for death and eternity? It is the Christians.

Yes, professed Christians sometimes do bad things. But it is infrequent enough to be newsworthy. If an atheist does a criminal act, it is to be expected. But, if a church leader does it, - it will make the headlines, because it is such a rare event.

What leads men to throw away the bottle and stop beating their wives? It is Christianity, not atheism. What saves the wayward girls, the teenage boys, and the rest of us out of lives of sin? It is Christianity, not atheism.

Christianity offers eternal happiness that begins now. Atheism can only offer doubt, skepticism, a miserable end, and eternal death.

Then the crowd turned to the atheist to give an answer, but he was gone. He had crept away without answering a word.

Vance Ferrell

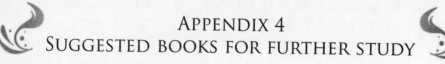

APPENDIX 4
SUGGESTED BOOKS FOR FURTHER STUDY

Blanchard, John. "Does God believe in Atheists?" Evangelical Press, 2000.

Comfort, Ray. "God Doesn't Believe in Atheists: Proof That the Atheist Doesn't Exist." Bridge-Logos Publishers, 2002.

Frame, John M. "Apologetics to the Glory of God." P & R Publishing, 1994.

Geisler, Norman. "I don't have enough Faith to be an Atheist." Crossway, 2004.

Hunt, Dave. "In Defense of the Faith." Harvest House Publishers, 1996.

Johnson, Phillip E. "Defeating Darwinism by Opening Minds." IVP, 1997.

Johnson, Phillip E. "Reason in the Balance: The Case Against Naturalism in Science, Law & Education." IVP, 1998.

Strobel, Lee. "The Case for a Creator." Zondervan, 2004.

Zacharia, Ravi. "Can man live without God?" World Publishing, 1994.

NUMERICAL REFERENCES

[1] As quoted by Pres. George Bush at Tsinghua University in China in 2002 see http://www.edu.cn/20020222/3020965.shtml

[2] See Appendix 1 for their testimonies.

[3] Jesus saith unto him, "I am the way, the truth, and the life; no man cometh unto the Father, but by me. (John 14:6)

[4] There have been more than 6.5 billion Bibles and New Testaments printed since the invention of the printing press in 1450 AD.

[5] Concise Oxford English Dictionary of Current English, Seventh edition, Clarendon Press, p.1109.

[6] Concise Oxford English Dictionary of Current English, p.54.

[7] E = mc2 Einstein demonstrated that all matter contains the same energy as cited by Gerald Schroeder, The Hidden Face of God, (Free Press, 2001), 25

[8] Thomas Nagel, The Last Word (OUP,1997),130.

[9] David Hume, On Human Nature and the Understanding (Collier Books, 1962),163.

[10] Stan Wallace, Does God Exist? The Craig-Flew Debate (Ashgate, 2002), 41

[11] Kai Nielsen, Reason and Practice: A modern Introduction to Philosophy (Harper & Row,1971), 48

[12] http://www.usatoday.com/sports/boxing/2005-06-12-tyson-retire-talk_x.htm

[13] Norman Geisler, I don't have enough Faith to be an Atheist (Crossway, 2004), 76

[14] Robert Jastrow, God and the Astronomers (W. W. Norton, 1978), 116.

[15] Arthur Eddington, Nature (Vol. 127, 1931), 450

[16] Arthur Eddington, The Expanding Universe (Macmillan,1933), 178

[17] Newsweek, Science Finds God, 7/20/98

[18] Anthony Flew renunciation in April 2005 http://www.christianitytoday.com/ct/2005/004/29.80.html

[19] Einstein, in a 1929 interview, in Denis Brian, Einstein: A Life (NY: J. Wiley, 1996), 186

[20] The fall of man and the curse of creation – see Genesis Chapter 1-3

[21] Charles B. Thaxton, The Mystery of Life's Origin: Reassessing Current Theories, (Philosophical Library, 1984)

[22] Norman Geisler, I don't have enough Faith to be an Atheist (Crossway, 2004), 117

[23] This tiny motor includes the equivalent of an engine block, a drive shaft, and three pistons. It is a variable speed motor that runs at speeds between 0.5 and 4.0 revolutions per second. The structure was discovered by John E. Walker from the MRC Laboratory of Molecular Biology, Cambridge, UK and he was awarded the Nobel Prize in Chemistry 1997.

[24] Franklin M. Harold, The Way of the Cell (OUP, 2001), 205

[25] Gerald Schroeder, The Hidden Face of God, (Free Press, 2001), 62

[26] Michael Denton, Evolution: Theory In Crisis (Adler, 1986), 264.

[27] One DNA strand is only 50 trillionths of an inch wide. If the DNA in all the cells of one person is strung out and placed end-to-end, it would extend from the sun to Jupiter and back about 118 times.

[28] Michael Denton, Evolution: A Theory in Crisis, (Adler, 1986), 338

[29] Phillip E. Johnson, Defeating Darwinism by Opening Minds, (IVP,1997), 73

[30] Interview with Dr. Gary Habermas http://www.biola.edu/antonyflew/

[31] Charles Darwin, The Origin of Species, p. 175.

[32] Http://www.ibm.com/news/us/en/2005/06/2005_06_23.html

[33] Around 360 thousand billion calculations per second — a speed known as 360 teraflops that some scientists say is comparable to the human brain

[34] Isaac Asimov, "In the Game of Energy and Thermodynamics You Can't Even Break Even," (Smithsonian, June 1970), 10.

[35] Carl Sagan, Cosmos, (Random House, 1980), 278

[36] Michael Denton, Evolution: A Theory in Crisis, (Adler, 1986), 330–331

[37] Prof. Dongarra cited http://www.cbsnews.com/stories/2002/11/19/tech/main530010.shtml

[38] Quote from correspondence with Jeffrey Zweerink, research physicist, UCLA October 2003 as cited in Norman Geisler, I don't have enough Faith to be an Atheist (Crossway, 2004), 102

[39] Stephen Hawking, A Brief History of Time (1988),125

[40] Hugh Ross, Why I am a Christian: Leading Thinkers Explain Why They Believe (Baker, 2001), 138

[41] Fred Hoyle, The Universe: Some Past and Present Reflections (University of Cardiff, 1982), 16

[42] Michael Behe, Darwin's Black Box (1996) 73 - for graphics and further examples see http://www.windowview.org/SCIENCE/32f.html

[43] William A. Dembski Still Spinning Just Fine: A Response To Ken Miller, 2.17.03 – see http://acs.ucsd.edu/~idea/dembski_flagellspin.htm

[44] Charles Darwin, The Origin of Species, p. 179.

[45] Carl Sagan, FH Crick and L.M. Mukhin, Extraterrestrial Life, (MIT Press, 1973).

[46] I. Prigogine, N. Gregair, A. Babbyabtz, Physics Today 25, 23-28

[47] Richard Dawkins, The Blind Watchmaker, (Norton, 1987),1

[48] F. Crick, What Mad Pursuit: A Personal View of Scientific Discovery, (Penguin Books 1990),138

[49] This quote by Roger Lewin was excerpted from Philip Whitfield, From So Simple A Beginning, (Macmillan, 1993), 7

[50] Richard Lewontin, review of Science as a Candle in the Dark by Carl Sagan, (New York review of Books, January 9,1997)

[51] Arthur Compton, 1927 Nobel Prize in Physics, (1936), Chicago Daily News.

[52] Margenau, H and R.A. Varghese, Cosmos, Bios, and Theos. (Open Court, 1992), 83.

53 F.J.Tipler, The Physics Of Immortality, (New York, 1994), Preface

54 abridged version of story in Can man live without God by Ravi Zacharias (World Publishing,1994), 182

55 Richard Dawkins, A Devil's Chaplain, (Mifflin, 2003), 248

56 www.yale.edu/lawweb/avalon/imt/proc/11-21-45.htm

57 C.S. Lewis, Mere Christianity, (Macmillan, 1952), 21

58 C.S. Lewis, Mere Christianity, (Macmillan, 1952), 19

59 Abridged from Norman Geisler, I don't have enough Faith to be an Atheist (Crossway, 2004), 174

60 Dave Hunt, In Defense of the Faith, (Harvest House Publishers, 1996), 41

61 Daily Telegraph, 4 February 1997.

62 Richard Dawkins, The Blind Watchmaker (Norton, 1987), 229

63 G.K. Chesterton, Orthodoxy (Doubleday, 1959), 41

64 Peter Singer, Practical Ethics, (Cambridge University, 1979), 122-123

65 Peter Berkowitz, Other Peoples Mothers?,New Republic, 10 January 2000

66 Http://www.lifesite.net/ldn/2006/nov/06112103.html

67 James Rachels, Created from Animals: The Moral Implications of Darwinism (OUP, 1990), 186

68 Dateline NBC program, on November 29, 1994.

69 See interview transcript http://www.answersingenesis.org/creation/v23/i4/rape.asp

70 Http://www.lifesite.net/ldn/2006/nov/06112103.html

71 Richard Dawkins, Book Review of Blueprints: Solving the Mystery of Evolution (New York Times, April 9, 1987), 34

72 John M. Frame, Apologetics to the Glory of God, P & R Publishing (February 1, 1994)

73 Interview in Lee Strobel, The Case for a Creator, (Zondervan, 2004), 264

74 Religion Today, <http://www.religiontoday.com/Archive/News Summary/>, November 2, 1999.

75 C. S. Lewis, Miracles, (Simon & Schuster, 1975), 23-4

76 Http://www.chinalaw.gov.cn/jsp/contentpub/browser/content proc.jsp?contentid=co265642723-

77 Cited by Saul K. Padover, Karl Marx: An Intimate Biography, (NAL), 280

78 Karl Sigmund et al., "The Economics of Fair Play," Scientific American, Vol. 286, January 2002, p. 87.

79 Cited in Knight's Treasury of 2,000 illustrations (Eerdmans,1992), 6

80 Richard Dawkins, A Devil's Chaplain, (Mifflin, 2003), 11

81 Isaiah 14:14 speaking of the fall of the devil from heaven

82 P.W. Atkins, The Creation, (WH Freeman & Co), 7

83 Http://catholiceducation.org/articles/science/sc0086.htm

84 As cited in http://www.answersingenesis.org/docs2001/1011news.asp

85 Richard Dawkins, The Blind Watchmaker, (Norton), 6

86 The entire debate can be viewed online at www.leaderu.com/offices/billcraig/docs/craig-atkins.html

87 Lee Strobel, The case for a Creator, (Zondervan, 2004), 277

88 Janet Daley, Daily Telegraph, 28 May 1996.

89 Http://tennessean.com/apps/pbcs.dll/article?AID=/20061129/NEWS06/611290429

90 Lillian Quigley, The Blind Men and the Elephant (Charles Scribner's Sons, 1959)

91 Http://www.biblesociety.org/index2.htm

92 Http://www.newyorker.com/printables/fact/061218fa_fact1

93 Is It True, Jews Win More Nobel Prizes Than Anyone Else?, The Jewish Press, Friday, May 9, 1997, Page 72.

94 Interview in Jerusalem Post with Gail Lichtman http://www.cuttingedge.org/news/n1076.html

95 For a more extensive treatment of this see http://www.answersingenesis.org/creation/v26/i1/hygiene.asp

96 Columbus's Journal reads "Who can doubt that this fire was not merely mine, but also the Holy Spirit who encouraged me with a radiance of marvelous illumination from his sacred Scriptures,... urging me to press forward?"

97 As quoted by James Moran of Harvard-Smithsonian Center for Astrophysics in Cambridge, Mass. – see http://www.chron.com/content/interactive/space/astronomy/news/1999/ds/990602.html

98 Http://www.solarviews.com/eng/sun.htm

99 As cited by Dave Hunt, In Defense of the Faith, (Harvest House Publishers), 74

100 John Blanchard, Does God believe in Atheists (Evangelical Press, 2000), 409

101 Compare 1 Kings 13:1-2 with 2 Kings 21:25-22:2 and 2 Kings 23: 15-18

102 Compare Isaiah 44:28 with Ezra 1:1-3

103 See Habakkuk 1:6-11

104 William F. Albright, Archaeology and the Religion of Israel, 176

105 A synthesis of Mohammed's personal prayers found in Sahih Bukhari Volume 8: #s 335, 379, 407, and 408, translated into English by Dr. Muhammad Muhsin Khan, at the Islamic University in Medina, published by Kitab Bhavan, New Delhi, India. For further references see http://answering-islam.org.uk/Silas/mo-sinner.htm

106 English translation of Holy Confucian Analects, Chapter 7

107 Gary Thomas, Christianity Today, October 3, 1994, 26.

108 Http://www.amitynewsservice.org/page.php?page=1251

109 Http://www.amitynewsservice.org/page.php?page=1649

A Note on the Type used in this Book

The body text of this book is set in *Baskerville,* a serif typeface designed in 1757 by John Baskerville, an English printer who took a holistic approach to printing. Not content with designing just typefaces, Baskerville made his own paper and ink. The typeface *Baskerville* is classified as a transitional typeface, positioned between the old style typefaces of William Caslon, and the modern styles of Giambattista Bodoni and Firmin Didot.

The header text is set in *Trajan Pro,* a serif typeface designed in 1989 by Carol Twombly for Adobe. The design is based on the letterforms of *capitalis monumentalis* or Roman square capitals, as used for the inscription at the base of Trajan's Column from which the typeface takes its name. Since lower case forms were not in use in Roman times, Trajan is an all-capitals typeface.

The subhead text is set in *Univers,* a realist sans-serif typeface designed by Adrian Frutiger in 1956. *Univers* takes inspiration from the 1896 typeface Akzidenz Grotesk. This typeface figures prominently in the Swiss Style of graphic design. The *Univers* type family consists of 14 weights plus 14 corresponding Oblique weights plus 16 variants with central European and Cyrillic character set. Different weights and variations within the type family are designated by the use of numbers rather than names, a system since adopted by Frutiger for other type designs.